BLUE
SKIES

BLUE SKIES

a traveler's journey of
discovery and life in Ukraine

Kat Rose

Blue Skies

Copyright © 2021 Kat Rose

Cover Design by C.S. Fritz

Formatting by Albatross Design Co.

All rights reserved under the Pan-American and International Copyright Convention. This book may not be reproduced in whole or in part, except for the brief quotations embodied in critical articles or reviews, in any form or by any means, electronic or mechanical, including photocopying, recording, or by any information storage and retrieval system now known or hereinafter invented, without permission of the author. Every effort has been made by the author to ensure that the information contained in this book was correct as of press time. The author hereby disclaims and does not assume liability for any injury, loss, damage, or disruption caused by errors or omissions, regardless of whether any errors or omissions result from negligence, accident, or any other cause. This book reflects the author's present recollections of experiences over time. Some names and characteristics have been changed to protect individuals' privacy, some events have been compressed, and some dialogue has been recreated based on the author's memory. The material in this publication is of the nature of general comment only and does not represent professional travel, health and safety advice. Readers are encouraged to verify any information contained in this book prior to taking any action on the information.

For permission requests, please contact anewerkatintown@gmail.com

ISBN (Paperback): 978-1-7368271-0-9

To My Sweet Poppy and to the Best "Guy."

*Thank you both for teaching me that life
is a beautiful journey.*

*"Eternal rest grant unto them, O Lord,
and let perpetual light shine upon them.
May the souls of all the faithful departed,
through the mercy of God, rest in peace."*

FOREWORD

The pages of this book are a journey of my life in Ukraine. What I write on these pages is not the history of Ukraine that is outlined in a detailed textbook. It is not stories of Ukrainian and Russian languages in the framework of a studied linguist. It is not Ukraine's latest news written by a professional journalist. It is not stories of cultural anthropology by a researcher who has dedicated his life's work to the study of Ukrainian culture. There are other books about each of these topics and I encourage you to read them.

Blue Skies is a collection of short stories written from my perspective as a young American living, working, and traveling throughout the country. It's not every traveler's experience or the experience of the people who live in Ukraine every day. It is my hope that these stories inspire personal reflection, travel to Ukraine, and international connection. Read between the lines and let the stories bring you a sense of hope, laughter, courage, and charity.

Thank you to my colleagues at Zhytomyr Ivan Franko State University, my students, my Fulbright cohort, the Ukraine Fulbright Commission, and others who made these stories come to life. Without your presence and encouragement, these stories would not have made it onto the following pages.

INTRODUCTION

I'm glad you're here. Maybe you're a Fulbright colleague, a friend of mine, a family member, a blog reader, or a stranger interested in travel and Ukraine. Somehow you've found out about this book, and it's a great joy to me that you've chosen to pick it up.

My name is Kat. I'm a girl in my twenties, living in New Jersey and dreaming of the next place I'll call home. I'm also the creator of the sustainable fashion and travel blog, *A Newer Kat in Town*. I started writing in 2015, after my first study abroad experience in the Czech Republic when I was nineteen. I was a miserable person back then. I only found joy in traveling. That led me to live in China in the summer of 2016, Italy for a year in 2016–2017, and Ukraine for the summers of 2018 and 2019. I traveled to thirty countries in Europe, Africa, and Asia throughout that time, each giving me their fix. I'd like to believe I'm a happier person now, but I suppose that depends.

I like to support my family, but I love to travel. I like to plan and have structure, but I love to dream. I like security, but I love to take risks and fall in love. My life is a dichotomy, two parallel lives vying for the same finite time: one wanting the comfort of home and the other wanting the joy of being on the road.

I am the youngest of my five sisters and six brothers. We are often referred to as "cheaper by the dozen." My mother is thirty-one years younger than my father, who was seventy-one when I was born. My father attended Columbia University, and my mother never attended college. He and my mother traveled around Europe and North America for my father's work and for the pure fun of seeing new places. My father was an engineer, a planner. My mother was a dreamer, a creative. Travel and do-it-yourself projects were always a big part of our lives. Maybe that's why I do what I do.

I've dreamed of being a travel writer since that first summer in the Czech Republic in 2015. I loved writing articles on my blog about travel, but I knew I wanted to write a book someday. I didn't think it would be a book of short stories, and I didn't think it would be about Ukraine.

I'm not Ukrainian-American. I didn't have Ukrainian connections before living there. I didn't study the Ukrainian language or Eastern European Studies in college. I encountered Ukraine as a volunteer at a small summer camp in a village in the western part of the country in 2018. I wanted to learn more about the language, the people, the war, and the culture, so I returned to Ukraine the following summer to the same summer camp and then as a Fulbright English Teaching Assistant in 2019–2020.

Ukraine is gritty, it's undiscovered, it's misunderstood, and it's a gem in Eastern Europe. It has its faults and its difficulties due to war and ununified identity. Yet, it captures a traveler in its hospitality, culture, and sense of curiosity. The stories you read in this book will illustrate each of those elements woven throughout my coming-of-age story during my time as a Fulbrighter in Ukraine. I was not Ukrainian then, and I am not Ukrainian now, but my journey with Ukraine is a narrative I'll continue to celebrate, and I'm happy that you're here to celebrate with me.

FALLING IN LOVE

On August 25, 2019, I moved to my fifth country: Ukraine. Chance had brought me here, but something else had kept me.

I fell in love.

I moved abroad for the first time when I was nineteen years old. I had been in an unhealthy relationship that had weighed me down for two years. When I arrived in my new city, I felt intense freedom and independence for the first time in years. I moved into my first apartment, made new friends, and traveled to different places around the world. I fell out of love with the person holding me back and into love with the newness of traveling.

When you go through a breakup, it's easy to wonder how life will move forward without that person. You see things that remind you of him or her. You wonder if you could've changed the outcome or if the situation was different, maybe you'd still be together. And sometimes, you're so clouded that you lose sight of who you are.

Traveling took all of that away from me. Booking the next trip became my fix. When I visited a new place, I was confident in who I was. I was filled with faith, curiosity, excitement, and purpose. I was happy.

As the months turned into years, I moved abroad three more times and visited more and more countries. I was on a high when I traveled and fell into an intense low when I returned home. The deep lows mimicked that breakup and only pushed me to go further the next time around.

I arrived in Ukraine and everything felt new again, a mirror of my nineteen-year-old self. I was learning a new language and navigating a new job with the freedom to engage with students in meaningful ways. I was seeing new cities that I had never heard of before. I was meeting new people from America and Ukraine who brought different perspectives into my life.

I fell in love with what traveling had given me time and time again.

People often ask me what I'm running away from each time I travel to a new destination. Moving to Ukraine was no different. I've thought about that question a lot over the years, even believing that it was true at times during my year in Ukraine. Yet, I've come to understand that statement as false. I certainly ran as I boarded my plane to Ukraine on that hot August day, but I didn't run away from my problems in America. I ran towards the feeling that travel gave me, a feeling that I knew I would experience in Ukraine. To me, it's the second closest feeling there is to falling in love.

PINCH ME

The airport was like any other, but I felt different. I was alone, and I could feel the ache of that aloneness throughout my entire body. I arrived in Kyiv, the capital of Ukraine, on September 5, 2019. I had spent the last ten days in the western city of Lviv with my Ukrainian friends that I had grown close to during the previous two summers. Lviv felt like any other quaint European city. It was comfortable, and I had a community there.

I sat in the backseat of my Uber, heading thirty-five minutes to the hotel where I would be staying for my Fulbright orientation from September 5–7. I wish I could say I was excited, but feelings of loneliness, fear, and guilt left no room for eagerness. I decided to come to Ukraine to teach university students, leaving my ninety-four-year-old father behind. I chose this adventure over my family and friends. I was doing to them what I had done again and again. I left them behind for the allure of travel.

Skyscrapers emerged in the distance as we neared the city center. I didn't have any expectations for what the city looked like; I hadn't Googled images of Kyiv before my arrival. I sat in the backseat wading in a mix of awe and shock as the bustling nature of a New York City rush hour weaved around me, 4600 miles away from the childhood city I was used to. The sidewalks were filled with commuters and young people; cafes were scattered on every street; buses and cars had created rows of traffic. I was naive or ignorant – I couldn't decide which – but I never imagined a city in Ukraine like the one before me.

I arrived at the twenty-story hotel, an accommodation higher than my standard of budget traveling. I rolled my suitcases to the check-in counter and handed my passport to the receptionist. I'm sure there were familiar faces in the lobby, and maybe I even said hello to them, but I was on auto-pilot: check-in, get your key, and go to your room.

I exited the elevator on one of the top floors and found my room. I slid the key into the lock, waiting anxiously to see who my roommate would be. I left my bags propped against the entranceway and took a deep breath, mentally preparing myself to make small talk after a long journey – 335 miles from Lviv to Kyiv.

I was met with a king bed and a beautiful view overlooking the city. *Pinch me, I was dreaming*. I had a room to myself for the next three days.

I was taking in the stillness of the room when my stomach pulled me out of my daze. I lost track of time and realized I hadn't eaten dinner. I knew my colleagues would probably be meeting up, but I needed time alone to recharge and process the whirlwind of emotions I had felt since leaving the familiarity of Lviv. I mapped the nearest supermarket and bought water, granola, and bananas. I was staying in a nice hotel, but that wouldn't change the budget traveler within me.

I slid my key into the lock, knowing this time that nobody was on the other side. I set down my groceries as the skyline drew my gaze to the window again. The sun was setting over the city, bringing with it city lights and a nightlife I was too tired to experience. I fell back onto the bed, surrendering myself to my new adventure and thanking God for this quiet blessing.

THE SAME LANGUAGE

I like the results of meeting new people, but I dislike the process. I don't like the beginnings of these relationships: small talk, big group activities, and cheesy ice-breakers. Maybe it's because I've always taken life a little too seriously, having grown up with a father who was seventy-one years older than me. Maybe it's because I overthink first impressions. Maybe it's because I'm often searching for a bigger purpose or a lesson in every experience.

It's one of my biggest faults: when conversations are boiled down to small talk, my mind tells me to run the other way. As I mentioned, I have five sisters and six brothers. The age gap between my parents is more than thirty years. I've lived in five countries and traveled to thirty others. How do you make these statements *small*?

It was September 6, the first day of our in-country orientation. I met the other awardees at our first orientation in Kansas in July before our arrival. I was quiet then and I was quiet now. I didn't speak much, but I did listen. I listened to the abbreviated stories of these new people, where they were from, what they were excited for, and what brought them to Ukraine.

We had a full day ahead of us: meetings about safety and health, about teaching English as a foreign language, and about resources from the U.S. Embassy. We boarded a coach bus headed to the first of these events at the Embassy. Another Fulbrighter was sitting next to me. The same type of conversation I had in Kansas and since arriving in Ukraine was on repeat. I wanted to get to know this person, but my mind wanted to hit fast-forward to the part where we were already friends.

Our day pressed on as we listened to different speakers and networked with international professionals. Yes, some part of me was excited about this new adventure, yet I couldn't silence the nagging voice in my mind reminding me of the comfort of my solo hotel room.

By evening, we arrived at our final event: a meet-and-greet with the U.S. Ambassador to Ukraine. I walked up to my roommate, who I shared a dorm with in Kansas, and asked her how she was enjoying orientation so far.

She sighed, "I'm exhausted. It's tiring talking to people all day, you know?"

This girl was speaking my language, and for the first time that day, I wanted to continue talking.

The crowds began to dwindle, a sign to say our goodbyes

and go from highly respected Fulbrighters to just being ordinary people. Orientation day one was complete. I got into an Uber with three other Fulbrighters. On our way back to the hotel, we drove through downtown Kyiv, passing Maidan and Saint Sophia's Cathedral.

As we drove past these new sites, previous trips flashed through my mind. A wheel of memories played of the adventures I had, the places I saw, and the people who became some of my best friends.

Those people became my best friends because I allowed myself to open up. I allowed myself to share my stories, my past, and my goals. This started as small talk – small talk as two strangers in a shared hostel room, as two people who grew up on opposite coasts of the United States or opposite sides of the world, as two people from different backgrounds who happened to meet in the same place.

If I could venture halfway across the world to Ukraine, then I could open my heart and mind to the new people around me, even if it meant beginning a new tomorrow with small talk.

ARE WE ALMOST THERE YET?

I had spent the last three days in Kyiv for our Fulbright orientation. It was September 7, and I was just getting used to being in a bustling city when it was time to move on. I stood at the entrance of the hotel with my new colleagues from the university where I would be teaching. Five hours prior, they were strangers to me. Now, we were making our way to my host city together.

I had three bags, no bus or train tickets, and a boatload

of fear. I didn't know how we would get to my host city of Zhytomyr, a city eighty-five miles west of Kyiv, or what my accommodation would be like. I didn't know what the city offered or what the university where I would be teaching for the next nine months would be like.

We took a taxi that brought us to a street lined with *marshrutkas*, or minibuses. Their respective destinations were written in Cyrillic. We walked to the one parked in front and I memorized my first Ukrainian word: Житомир (Zhytomyr). The driver helped me load my bags and we took our seats in the front.

There are a series of moments I believe many travelers and adventurers around the world encounter. You start out eager as you begin planning your life-changing trip. You pack and a wave of sadness hits as you say goodbye to your friends and family. Your excitement returns as you board your plane. It isn't until you arrive at your destination alone that a flash of reality hits you and you wonder, "What am I doing here?"

The driver turned the key in the ignition. *What am I doing here? Why did I choose to come to Ukraine? How would I live alone in a place where I didn't have friends or family?* Questions of fear churned in my mind as I fronted a smile and continued to make small talk with my colleagues.

Time feels slow when you don't have a sense of direction in an unfamiliar place. We passed village after village, field after field. I felt like we had been driving for hours. Like a child on a road trip, I turned and asked my colleague, "Are we almost there yet?"

I looked out the window. I saw a sunflower field showcasing thousands and thousands of blooming golden flowers. The sun was setting in the backdrop, reflecting the flowers and filling the sky with a mix of pastel colors: orange, yellow, and purple. Behind us, a green forest of perfectly lined pine trees was fading into the dusk. I breathed in deeply, and my mind quieted for the first time since we departed. It was the end of summer, the start of what would become an unforgettable adventure.

PRAYER OF KINDNESS

The kindness you expressed to me was a type of compassion words can't describe. We had lived separate lives, thousands of miles drawn between us. You were from Ukraine and I was from America. I didn't know much about Zhytomyr, the city that I would live in for the next nine months. You had built a life and a family there. You graduated from and taught English at the university where I would soon begin my Fulbright English Teaching Assistantship.

We sat across from one another as strangers at our first meeting in Kyiv. I was rambling one question after the other, and you patiently answered each one.

"Do you know of any vacant apartments?"

"What classes will I be teaching?"

"What are the students like?"

"What are your favorite things to do in the city?"

With each answer, I wondered how you came to be my contact, helping me adjust to life in Ukraine and navigate my new role as a teaching assistant. I wondered if you volunteered, if everyone else was too busy, or if I was assigned to you.

I was surprised when your husband and daughter met us at the bus station when we arrived in Zhytomyr. Your husband smiled and eagerly helped with my bags before I could even introduce myself. Your daughter hugged me and gave me a handwritten welcome. You and your family made my temporary room homier, bringing me fresh cucumbers and tomatoes, cookies, tea, towels, and bedding. That night has a special place in my heart; I was a stranger, and you welcomed me into your family from the start.

Over the next few days, you guided me around Zhytomyr. You showed me the pedestrian street with the blue church, introduced me to my new colleagues and the dean of the university, and searched for apartments with me, even offering to let me live in your mother's vacant flat. In each of those moments, you helped me build the foundation of my new adventure.

As I gained confidence, you continued to support me. You asked me how my lessons were, eager to invite me to your classes and allow me to teach your students. You asked me about my visits to other Ukrainian cities. You asked me about my family and upbringing in America, and when I was lonely and homesick, you invited me over for dinner and coffee. You didn't just get to know me as the *American*, you knew me for *me*.

In the weeks that turned into months, I found myself wondering how two strangers ended up building a relationship and becoming like family. The only answer I could come up with was kindness.

When I think about Ukraine, I think about those acts of kindness from people that used to be strangers to me, people that welcomed me into their country, their homes, and their lives. I think about how different my experience would've been without those moments. You used to be one of those strangers, and only now do I understand the power of what you taught me. You taught me to be as kind to others as you were to me. That's a prayer I'll keep praying until we meet again.

A SEARCH FOR HOME

I arrived in Zhytomyr on September 7 without a permanent place to sleep; it was easier to search for an apartment upon arrival rather than commit to an apartment online and sight unseen.

We arrived late in the evening. The unfamiliar streets were dark, and the sun was long gone. I was nervous, and I could feel the loneliness gnawing at me as we pulled up to a grey concrete building.

The building was home to the student dorms. Since I didn't have my own apartment, this was the best option in the interim. Staying for two weeks at the dorm cost twenty dollars and gave me a bed, a bathroom, and a pseudo-kitchen.

My Ukrainian students from Lviv had warned me that dorms in Ukraine were very old and often ridden with plumbing, pest, and hygiene issues. I took what they said with a grain of salt; the dorms couldn't be that bad.

I saw both run-down dorms in my subsequent trips to Ukrainian universities and more modern ones. The dorm I stayed in that night had its issues, falling somewhere in the middle of run-down and renovated. I won't go into detail so as not to offend my community there.

What I will say is that I spent the night sleeping on top of my two suitcases that I had placed in a line to form a "bed." Before the sun rose, I was up and searching for Airbnbs near the city center. I booked an apartment for the next six days. It cost 250 dollars, the cost of what my future apartment would be *per month*.

Six days. That was the number of days I had to find an apartment in a foreign city where I didn't speak the language or know anyone besides Irena, my contact who had met me at orientation.

Two powerful and outspoken Ukrainian women, who were professors at my university, walked five feet ahead of me. No matter how hard I tried to keep up, I fell behind. Whether I could keep up or not, they were on a mission to help me find a new home in Zhytomyr.

When Elena's phone rang, Luda's phone rang shortly after. They spoke to one realtor after another for three days to help me find a vacant one-bedroom apartment. They spoke clearly and strong-willed to each other and to each realtor, giving their opinions and making sure I would not be ripped off or met with surprises in my flat. They were like two mothers watching out for me, and for that, I was filled with gratitude.

We saw old apartments and newly renovated ones. We saw apartments on the fifth floor of old Soviet buildings with no hot water after five o'clock in the evening, apartments that didn't have washing machines, and apartments with families still living there, their clothes and belongings in each nook.

One apartment we looked at was a block away from Elena's flat, which was across the street from the local market and a fifteen-minute walk to the university. It was a small one-bedroom flat, comfortable for one person, and could accommodate one or two guests. We saw it on our first day.

Although I wanted to continue searching, the realtor told me I needed to decide if I wanted to rent it within forty-eight hours.

And so on the third day of our search, I became the proud renter of my first international apartment in a small corner of Zhytomyr – a city I didn't choose, a city that would present its opportunities and challenges, a city that would be filled with memories, laughter, and loads of surprises.

UNWELCOME VISITORS

I paid the deposit on my apartment on September 11. The keys were in my hand. It would be my little home for the next nine months. A feeling of satisfaction and peace radiated throughout my body. I was living in my first solo apartment.

My contact, Irena, and her husband kindly helped me move my suitcases into the new flat. I had two suitcases and a carry-on bag, plus some basic groceries. They gave me the afternoon to unwind.

The owners had informed me that someone was taking care of the place before me, but a thick film of dust and dirt covered the apartment. The floors, the wardrobe, the living space, the bathroom, and especially the kitchen needed to be cleaned.

My groceries were sitting on the table, so I decided to start with the kitchen. I opened the cabinet under the sink to see if there was a garbage bin. An itch shot down my spine as I watched a long-tailed creature scuttle into a hole behind the pipes.

I slammed the cabinet door shut as quickly as I opened it.

I wondered if the realtor knew about the mice and if that's why I had to make a decision so quickly.

I didn't want to be unappreciative for my new apartment, but I also needed to find someone who could potentially point me in the direction of an exterminator. I spoke with Irena and asked if there was one we could call.

She responded, confused, "What's an exterminator?"

I discovered something new that day: the job of an exterminator didn't exist.

The following day, the news spread to Elena, who thankfully only lived a block away. She arrived at my door holding the oldest mouse trap I had ever seen – a dark plank of jagged wood with a snapback and pin. She realized by the look on my face that I was expecting something very different.

She walked into the kitchen unfazed as she said in a maternal voice, "Here's how you use it. We'll put the cheese here and hook it to the metal part. When the mouse eats it, the trap will release."

One hour later, I heard a snap. I cringed, and the same itch ran down my spine as I nervously opened the cabinet door. The trap had worked; in it laid a dead mouse. I called my colleague to thank her, assuming the problem was fixed. I would simply dispose of the mouse and the trap along with it. Much to my surprise, ten minutes later, she arrived at my door saying we had to set up the trap again to make sure there were no more mice.

I stood in shock. We were going to remove the dead mouse and reuse the same trap. I tried as best as I could to muster up the courage to remove the mouse from the trap, but I couldn't do it.

Elena laughed and said, "I'll help you."

Snap! The story replayed. She removed the mouse and we set the trap for the third time. *Snap*! I cringed again. This time, however, Elena was teaching a class and couldn't come. I left the mouse under the sink, thinking, "Kat, you can travel solo around the world, but you can't get yourself to touch a dead mouse?"

That evening, the owner of the flat arrived to set up the new refrigerator. He noticed the open cabinet in the kitchen and saw the dead mouse. I didn't have a chance to speak before he picked up the trap and removed the mouse with his bare hands. I discovered something else that day: either I was a coward or Ukrainians had a form of resilience that I was only beginning to understand.

UNWELCOME VISITORS, TAKE TWO

The mice were bearable in comparison to what else was cohabitating in my apartment.

On move-in day, as I was cleaning the apartment, I noticed a few bugs. No problem, I had already been part of a mice extermination process, thanks to Elena. I could keep my big girl pants on and kill a few bugs.

One, two, three killed.

It made sense that there were some critters in my new apartment; no one had been living here for quite some time. Plus, there could be bugs and mice in any apartment in any city in the world. It wasn't a problem unique to Ukraine.

My big girl pants didn't last very long. As my first few days turned into a week, I realized that I didn't just have a few bugs in my apartment; I had a cockroach infestation.

I had never experienced living with cockroaches before. They lived in my kitchen, not the bathroom, not the hallway, not the bedroom. I would open a cabinet and one would scurry away. I'd move a dish and one would run behind the sink. I'd look up and see one crawling near the ceiling light.

Cockroaches come out when the lights are off and there isn't much noise. You couldn't pay me enough money to walk in that kitchen when it was dark. In the early morning, I would open the cabinets slowly, inspect the table and underside, and scan the sink area. I'd kill two or three almost every day.

Discomfort is not a strong enough word to describe my experience living with cockroaches. I couldn't stand being in my kitchen. I couldn't eat there and or do work at the kitchen table.

I felt bad bringing up my apartment issues with my colleagues. I just got unlucky with an apartment that had a few (or more) kinks, let's say.

Week after week, a colleague would generously bring me a new cockroach killer: a spray, a paste, a trap.

For a few days, I wouldn't see any cockroaches. Just when I thought the coast was clear, another would reappear, and the cycle would start again.

I hesitated writing a story about having cockroaches in my apartment. There are modern apartments throughout Ukraine without pests. It had nothing to do with the owners or with living in Ukraine. In fact, the owners and my colleagues did everything they could to improve the situation.

That's why I wrote this story. Ukrainians are selfless, they are kind, and they will go above and beyond to help you, whether you ask or not. That was my experience with the apartment search, the mice, and the cockroaches, as well as the lesson planning, the many travels, and the stories that are woven throughout this book. To be like Ukrainians is to serve those in need, to extend a helping hand, and to bring hospitality into conversation and experiences with others. The cockroaches may have been a thorn in my life every time I entered my kitchen, but Ukrainian hospitality and kindness were the roses that made the thorns a little easier to bear.

GOODNIGHT MOON

When we were negotiating the rent for my flat, my colleagues asked the owners if they could provide a bed since there wasn't one in the apartment. The owners didn't have an extra bed, but they agreed to purchase one for me or subtract the cost of a bed from my first month's rent payment.

I opted for the latter so I could choose my own bed. I needed a place to sleep, so the mission to find a bed was on full-speed ahead. My colleague informed me of a website called OLX, similar to the U.S. site, Craigslist. Among other features, people can post used or new furniture by location.

Some people may think it's unhygienic to use a secondhand bed, but I figured I had slept on countless hostel beds over the years, and I could buy a mattress cover. Plus, if the bed wasn't clean, I could keep the frame and just buy a new mattress.

I found a twin bed for forty dollars on OLX that appeared to be in good condition. My flat owners gave me a discount of about 100 dollars, so I had extra money if I wanted to buy a new mattress. I copied the link and sent it to Irena to ask for her opinion. She thought it looked like a promising option and called the owner; he was happy to meet us in his village. We took a fifty-cent sweltering bus ride to a small village on the outskirts of the city. As we walked down a dirt road trying to find the number of the house he had given us, sweat dripped down my back. The sun beat down on us and the late September flowers.

An older Ukrainian man was waiting by a gate with the number we were searching for. The man, along with his wife, welcomed us into their house to see the bed. The mattress was clean, hardly used, and exactly what I was looking for. I noticed two large glass jars sitting on a wooden table in the room where the bed was. They were filled with fruit and a dark liquid that had begun to pool at the bottom of the jar. I gestured to the table and asked Irena if she could ask the owners what they were making. The owners smiled at my curiosity, and before I knew it, I was given a small teacup of the dark red liquid.

"Be careful, it will get you drunk quickly," Irena translated.

It was homemade cherry wine, and it was one of the sweetest wines I had ever tasted. I sipped the wine, finding joy in trying something new and witnessing Ukrainian culture and hospitality. These are the moments that travelers seek, the authentic moments you can't find on a tour or in a guidebook. They are real people showing you real-life – something I couldn't have found if I let the owners of my flat buy me a bed.

I handed forty dollars and the empty cup to the owners

with gratitude for sharing with me. We walked outside together and they gave us a tour of their majestic garden filled with roses and different types of apple trees. As we wandered through the garden, our taxi driver arrived in a small van. It didn't look big enough to fit my new bed, but I was learning quickly that Ukrainians always find a way to make unlikely situations work out.

The two men carried the bed outside and slid it into the back of the van. The back doors couldn't close, so the driver tied a thin rope around the handles, the only thing keeping the bed from sliding out. We thanked the couple again and said goodbye.

There were two seats in the front of the van: one for the driver and one that I assumed Irena and I would share. The driver sat in the front seat, and Irena climbed into the back of the van and sat on top of the bed. I couldn't believe she was going to sit on top of the bed with the doors wide open as we drove back to the city center.

"Let's go. We did it!" Irena said, unfazed.

I climbed into the front seat and the driver began our way back to my apartment. The wind was blowing and Irena was bouncing with the springs of the bed at every bump. I was tipsy on cherry wine and high on life.

FEELING BLUE

Each year, the city celebrates "Zhytomyr Day" the second weekend in September. It's a day filled with food stands, shows, a mini carnival, and handmade crafts. Luda, one of the women who helped me find my apartment, invited me to celebrate with her. I was overwhelmed with furnishing an apartment solo and was grateful for an invitation to join the community.

The sky was bright blue, and the crisp air signaled a hint of fall. Luda and I met at the university. Just as she and Elena had walked with purpose to each apartment, Luda continued to power walk around the city, showing me sites I hadn't yet seen.

We saw the central park and the pedestrian bridge, a bridge that crosses the river and connects Zhytomyr to the nearby villages.

Luda was older than me, maybe in her fifties or sixties (you can never really tell the age of Ukrainian women). I enjoyed spending the day with her as we talked about Zhytomyr, the university, and cooking. I asked her lots of questions about food. I wanted to learn more about Ukrainian cuisine, pickling, and tradition.

She told me that she loved to cook a particular dish with a blue vegetable. As she was telling me about the dish, in the back of my mind, I thought of every vegetable I knew of. I couldn't think of a blue vegetable.

I interrupted her, "Wait, what vegetable are you talking about?"

"The blue one!" she said confidently.

I smiled, politely saying, "I don't know any blue vegetables."

We spent the next ten minutes sitting on a park bench, listing every vegetable we could think of. None of them were blue.

"Баклажан!" she repeated over and over again, trying to think of the English translation.

Luda Google translated the word. It came up as squash.

That wasn't blue. I even Googled blue vegetables with no luck.

I was hungry for lunch, so we walked back to the food stands in the city center. I was vegetarian, so there wasn't much for me to eat except a few grilled vegetables and potatoes, the usual in Ukraine. I pointed to the vegetables that I wanted, asking Luda for the translation so I could order.

"Баклажан!" she shouted.

I looked at the platter of grilled vegetables. The mystery was solved! The infamous blue vegetable was, in fact, an eggplant.

We laughed even harder as I took a bite of the eggplant and said, "This isn't a blue vegetable, Luda. It's purple!"

She explained that the colloquial word for eggplant at the market is called "Синій," meaning blue. I had my first Ukrainian language lesson that day. Thanks to Luda, I will never forget the Ukrainian word for eggplant.

COVERED IN PLAIN SIGHT

Purchasing a bed was the number one priority during the move-in process. With the help of Irena, a kind village couple, and some cherry wine on top, I had a new bed sitting in my room, fitted with bright yellow sheets borrowed from a colleague.

The second priority was purchasing bath towels and a shower curtain. Irena had kindly given me a towel from her home to use while I was staying at the dorm, but it needed to be washed after a few days, and I wanted to purchase a few extras for guests. I also needed a shower curtain so my bathroom wouldn't turn into a flood zone like it had the nights prior. The previous shower curtain was grimy and now sat in the dumpster outside my flat.

It couldn't be that hard to buy a few towels and a shower curtain, I thought to myself as I walked to a small store I had passed a few times on my way to the university.

I picked out three light pink towels and a pink floral shower curtain. Easy peasy.

I returned home to my apartment, attached the new shower curtain to the metal rod, and hung up the new towels on the hooks in the bathroom.

I was excited to take a shower that night; I had a bright pink shower curtain that elevated the outdated bathroom and matching towels waiting to be used. Plus, I wouldn't have to mop up the bathroom after my shower.

I turned on the handheld showerhead and stepped into the tub. In an ideal world, the shower curtain would stick to the bathtub, keeping the water inside the tub. But, I wasn't living in an ideal world. The shower curtain clung to every inch of my wet body, not only making it impossible to shower, but also flooding my bathroom yet again.

My shower was over as quickly as it had started. I reached for the faucet handle and turned off the showerhead. Pink puddles of water pooled around my feet, staining the old white bathtub. I peeled the wet shower curtain from my damp body. In its place were pink dye marks and splotches where the curtain had wrapped around me. My pink skin and the pink bathtub matched.

I grabbed my new pink towel, almost slipping on the wet tile floor. I wiped my face, my torso, my arms, my legs, and my back.

The more I dried myself, the worse the problem became. Not only was my skin stained pink from the shower curtain, but I was now covered in a film of pink lint from the cheap towel. Every inch of my body had minuscule pieces of pink fiber, the water on my body acting as a glue for the fabric.

I stood in my flooded bathroom, bewildered, naked, and pink. I had a few options: I could shower again to remove the lint and risk getting more dye on me, I could continue to dry myself with lint, or I could stand naked in my apartment and let my body air dry.

Two shower curtains sat in my dumpster, my bathtub remained pink (even to this day and after scrubbing it), and I was back to square one.

I walked into a different shop, choosing a more expensive shower curtain, one that *wasn't* pink.

A SMALL WORLD

When I began searching for appliances and furnishings for my apartment, I wanted to shop secondhand. Whatever I couldn't buy used, I would then buy locally from small businesses. I learned that this was much easier to accomplish in Ukraine than in the United States, a country ridden with chain stores. While there are some big-box stores in Ukraine, much of the economy relies largely on small businesses that sell one type of product. For example, if you need a rug for your bedroom, you go to the carpet store. If you need soil for your plants, you go to the garden store. If you need an extension cord, you go to the electronics store.

After my many bathroom floods, I needed a bath mat, so I went to the bathroom store. I wandered through the maze of the local market across from my new flat. I was intimidated by hundreds of sellers calling out to me. My physical features blended in with the local people, but I still wondered if they could tell I wasn't from their country. I passed a few storefronts mixed in with the array of fruit and veggie stands. Some stores looked like they would have bathroom supplies, but I wasn't confident enough to go in. I reached a dead-end, passing a row of stores on my right. The final store had bath mats hanging in the window.

I gave myself a pep-talk, "Kat, just go in and buy what you need."

I walked in and was met by a young blonde woman with a smile. She spoke to me in Russian, and I could feel the sweat dripping down my back. I kindly asked her if she spoke English. She hesitated before responding; she studied English for a few years but told me she wasn't very good at speaking. I didn't care how long she studied or how well she could speak; I was relieved to meet someone who I could communicate with. I had chosen the right store.

We chatted for ten or fifteen minutes. I learned that her name was Larysa. She extended her sincere welcome and asked me what had brought me to Zhytomyr. I explained that I was here to teach English and had just moved into an unfurnished apartment nearby. As other customers entered the store, our conversation trailed off. I bought a bath mat, thanked her, and returned to my apartment, feeling proud that I had accomplished a small task in an unfamiliar city.

A few days later, I realized I still needed a few items for my apartment: a garbage can for the bathroom and one for the kitchen. I thought I had seen those items in the bathroom store. I weaved my way back to the same dead end.

I met Larysa and she smiled, as excited to see me as I was to see her. Before I could say anything, she pulled out her phone and stepped outside to make a call. As I wandered around the store, Larysa came back in saying, "My friend is on the phone. She wants to talk to you."

I stuttered, not knowing how to tell her that I wasn't comfortable talking to a stranger on her phone. She could sense my hesitation and, trying to make me feel comfortable, said, "She's an English teacher like you."

I paused for a minute before agreeing to pick up the phone. I traveled to Ukraine. I was living in this small foreign city. I decided to live in an unfurnished apartment. I might as well talk.

I put the phone up to my ear, "Hello?"

Her name was Iryna. She was a Zhytomyr native who ran an English school in the city. She admitted that the situation was strange, but that she would like to meet me. Larysa was one of her previous students and had informed her that she met an American English teacher living in Zhytomyr for a year. I was taken aback by the situation; I was just trying to buy some garbage cans when I was cornered in a conversation. I decided to give Iryna my email and told her to email me more information about her school.

I smiled at Larysa as I walked out the door with my garbage cans, wondering if I chose the right store after all.

A SMALLER WORLD

An email chain between Iryna and I sat in my inbox. After our short phone conversation and emails, I trusted her intention in meeting me. Her English school was legitimate, as was her genuineness.

I clicked on the latest unread email from Iryna. We planned to meet at ten o'clock in the morning on September 25. She informed me of our meeting point, a monument in the city center. From there, she would show me a coffee shop where we could chat.

There was only one problem; I didn't know where the monument was. I had only been living in Zhytomyr for a little over two weeks. I Googled the monument's name in English, but no results came up.

It was 9:45, fifteen minutes before our meeting time. I didn't have Iryna's phone number, so I emailed her again asking for an exact address. The clock neared ten. I checked my email again.

Her email read, "I'm already at the monument. I will meet you at Larysa's store. Wait for me there."

I was relieved that she understood that I wasn't trying to stand her up. I laughed to myself again at the unlikely scene unfolding before me: I was on my way to Larysa's store for the third time that week, a store that I had only chosen to enter because bath mats were hanging in the window. I arrived at the store, coming face to face with the mysterious woman who somehow discovered I existed in this small corner of the world.

She was a woman in her mid-life with striking dark features and an aura that exuded confidence and wisdom.

She smiled eagerly and introduced herself to me. I apologized for veering from our original meeting point when she interrupted me, "Don't worry about it, I'm the crazy one who asked you to meet me."

I followed her lead as she navigated her way through the maze of the market with ease, guiding us to an open street with a cozy cafe. We ordered two Americanos. I tried to pay for my own, but she insisted on treating me. You can try to compete with Ukrainian hospitality, but know that you will always lose.

We sat and sipped our coffee. I learned that she graduated from the university where I was teaching English. She had traveled extensively and spent six years living in the United Arab Emirates as a solo female. She returned to Ukraine and launched a successful English school. With each discovery, I understood why my first impression of her was of a woman with confidence and in-depth knowledge.

I admired her travel and entrepreneurial spirit, accompanied by her bold attitude towards meeting strangers. I shared my story with her and how I ended up in Ukraine. I told her how I chose an unfurnished apartment, that I wanted to start studying the Ukrainian language, and that I was searching for a gym to join and activities in the local community to participate in.

Without hesitation, she suggested that she could teach me Ukrainian. I was grateful for her offer since I hadn't found a tutor yet. When I asked how much her rate was, she chuckled and, with a smile, said, "I want to teach you for free."

What was the catch? Why did she want to help a stranger for free? I couldn't accept her offer without payment, but she insisted that she wanted to help me. I suggested that I could volunteer at her school in exchange.

I was amazed by what occurred during our conversation: the world was a small place, and was even smaller when two strangers extended kindness and service. There was no maliciousness or ill-intent, just two people using their free time and knowledge to help one another.

My mind was caught up in the mystery of our meeting when she added, "And by the way, I'd love for you to join our workout classes on Saturdays. I'll meet you there this weekend."

SILVER PLATTER

My first priority was to purchase a bed, the second was to purchase a bath towel and shower curtain (an attempt that ended up taking three tries), and the third was to purchase kitchenware.

The kitchen was empty when I arrived, not a single pot, plate, fork, knife, or cup – not even a refrigerator. I recall eating out and snacking those first few days – lots of coffee, cookies, dark chocolate, and peanut butter.

My colleagues had graciously lent me a few teacups and plates, but there was much more to buy. Utensils, chopping boards, cups, bowls, pots, pans, cutting knives, storage containers, oven mitts, dish towels, and baking sheets. The list was overwhelming.

I spent three days searching for and buying everything I needed from local kitchen stores.

Having already purchased a bed and still needing other furniture for my apartment, I didn't want to spend a lot of money on kitchen supplies. I also knew I would only be in this flat for nine months.

Two pots and a frying pan sat on my stove. I didn't have any idea how much these items usually cost, but I thought they were affordable for Ukraine: ten dollars for each pot and twelve dollars for the frying pan.

I was content. My drawers were filled with utensils and my cabinets were filled with cups and bowls. I was ready to prepare my first home-cooked meal.

I was cooking rice in the pot as the tofu was frying in the pan, waiting for veggies, ginger, and soy sauce to be added. I grabbed my new spatula and flipped the tofu.

I stood bewildered, but at least I wasn't naked and pink this time. The top metal layer of the frying pan was no longer on the pan; it had molded to my tofu. Metal flakes remained on my new spatula.

I threw the pot and coveted tofu in the trash and went out to eat for dinner yet again. I don't know which item I was more upset about discarding: the tofu or the frying pan, each taking multiple trips to find.

The following day, I power walked through the maze of the market to a store near Larysa's that sold pots and pans. By now, I didn't have any fear. I had been dyed pink and covered in lint. I had killed mice and cockroaches. I drank homemade cherry wine, and I met a friend and a Ukrainian tutor by buying a bath mat. I walked into the store with confidence, a woman on a mission, and asked for the most expensive, highest-quality cast iron skillet that she sold.

It was expensive, very expensive, but it didn't matter. I learned that quality is greater than quantity, and patience is greater than immediate gratification.

TWO STEPS BEHIND

Iryna texted me the address of the fitness center where she took weekly classes. Since I opened my big mouth and said I wanted to get more involved in the community and I wanted to be more active, I had no one else to blame but myself for having to wake up at 6:30 in the morning to meet Iryna at the gym by 7:15 on a Saturday morning.

Iryna had already impressed me with her solo international travels and poise, but to hear that she took a fitness class at that hour three times a week was even more impressive.

I signed up for twenty classes: about three per week. If Iryna could commit, I could too.

Iryna was like the cool Ukrainian aunt I never had. She introduced me to the fitness instructor, who was kind and welcoming. She also introduced me to the usual crowd in the locker room, where everyone was changing into their gym clothes; I already had my workout clothes on.

I quickly realized that Ukrainians wear regular clothes to the gym, change into workout clothes there, and then change back into their regular clothes to go home. I didn't care how many stares I received or how many people told me I would get sick in the cold winter months from walking outside wearing sweaty clothes, I was not wasting my time changing. There were some American cultural norms I had to stick to and that was one of them.

It was already obvious that I was American by my clothing choices, and even more obvious when the class began. The first class was the hardest since I couldn't understand the teacher's directions. I tried my best to follow Iryna and the other women in the class, but I was two steps behind for *everything.*

There was nothing I could do but laugh at myself and keep going. Here I was taking a fitness class with a woman I met through a woman I happened to buy a bath mat from in a store I happened to walk into.

When the class was over, I couldn't stop smiling. I was proud of myself for taking the class. It takes courage to be vulnerable and try new things in a new environment. If I could take a fitness class in a foreign language, I had the courage to do much more.

That "much more" included my first Ukrainian language lesson with Iryna. I kept my workout clothes on while Iryna changed into regular clothes. We walked to the nearest cafe where we ordered coffee and found a table to sit at for the next hour.

To say I was nervous was an understatement. I studied Italian for a year while living in Italy, but that was three years ago. I hadn't studied a new language since then. I questioned myself, having planted the seeds of doubt after comparing myself to other Fulbrighters whose language skills were far more advanced than mine.

We started with the alphabet – I felt like a Kindergartener learning my ABCs – then we continued with basic greetings and phrases. Iryna was patient. She was thorough in her explanations, she spoke clearly, and she didn't judge me. She showed me what an effective and kind teacher looks like. Over the next several months, I would learn more than just Ukrainian from her; I would look to her example as I taught my students and learned to be a teacher myself.

TELL THEM YOU LOVE RUNNING

After one of my brothers passed away in 2016, running became a tool for me. When I started running, the discomfort took me out of my grief. My physical pain outweighed my emotional pain. I could let my mind rest and allow my body to do the hard work. Over time, I began to like running and even started running half-marathons. I could run distances anywhere as long as I had my sneakers and the right playlist. Turn the music on, turn my thoughts off, and put one foot in front of the other.

When I arrived in Zhytomyr, I had the same mindset: as long as I had my sneakers and the right playlist, I could run anywhere. I allowed myself a grace period of two weeks as I settled into my apartment. I wouldn't worry about running and adding one more thing to my to-do list. During those weeks, I met with the dean of my university. She asked me to prepare a list of goals that I wanted to achieve during my time in Ukraine.

On that list, I wrote: *run a half-marathon and full marathon in Ukraine.*

I had dreamed of running a half-marathon in each of my colleagues' host cities, which would mean racing once per month. I had trained for a half-marathon in New York City six months prior and failed at mile ten. I pushed too hard and led myself down a path of injury. It required months of physical therapy to recover. My mind wanted to run more in Ukraine, but my body knew one half-marathon and one full marathon would be fulfilling.

The dean read my goals aloud, pausing when she reached the one about running.

She repeated my goal with a mix of disbelief and surprise.

I wanted to shut down any doubt that crept into the space between us. I blurted out, "I love running."

My alarm blared at 5:30 the following Sunday morning on September 29. My apartment was cold; a signal that the seasons had changed. I pulled the covers off and felt the cold air hit me. I mumbled, "This is what I get for telling them I love running," as I put on my running clothes and an extra layer. I grabbed my headphones, laced up my sneakers, and locked the door behind me.

It was still dark out as I walked past the market towards the park. I was meeting a group of local runners, one of whom was a professor at the university named Oleg. Word spread from the dean that there was a girl interested in running marathons in Ukraine, and he was the go-to running guy. One thing led to the next, and here I was standing nervously in front of him and a group of dedicated Ukrainian runners.

I smiled as I introduced myself to the group. I quickly realized that the members of the group high-five each other when they meet, so I did that too. Many didn't speak English, but I was grateful for their warm and friendly welcome and the ability to explore running trails with locals who knew them well. With the help of Oleg's translations, they asked me how I became interested in running in America and how many marathons I had run. I was happy to answer and hear their responses too. I didn't reveal that this was my first time running since my injury six months prior.

My feet hit the mix of dirt and gravel beneath me, one foot in front of the other. I avoided holes and rocks as I worked to keep pace with the group of runners leading the way.

As long as I had my sneakers and the right playlist, I could run anywhere. It felt good to be doing what I loved again.

SPINNING IN CIRCLES

Karma was a bitch, or Ukraine was playing a joke on me. After the first two or three weeks of adjusting to the nuances and daily surprises of life in Ukraine, I began to feel more confident. I had furnished an apartment, taken my first Ukrainian language lesson, and began to make plans at the university. Things seemed to be on the up.

From my previous travels, I knew there would be a few weeks where I felt off; others might call this period "culture shock." I was walking home from a trip to the market, feeling lighter than I had in the previous weeks. The shock was wearing off. This was my new home and I was establishing my place here.

I arrived in my apartment, cooked dinner, and started planning for the rest of the week. I did an at-home yoga class and got ready for the night. As I was changing into my pajamas, I noticed the mound of laundry in the corner of my room that I had been ignoring. I picked up the pile of clothes and fit what I could into my tiny, European-sized washing machine in my kitchen. I put the detergent in and pressed whatever buttons managed to get the thing started.

I walked back to my couch to answer some emails when I was met with yet another surprise.

My apartment went black.

I try not to curse, but every curse word I knew came out of my mouth at that moment. I fumbled around, cussing, as I couldn't find my phone to use the flashlight. I made my way through the dark to the kitchen, where I knew there was a pack of matches by the stove. I lit one and walked to the hallway to find the fuse box. Bingo, I found the box and saw a red button. I hesitated as the hot flame inched closer to my finger. Either the match was going to burn my finger, I was going to get electrocuted, or I would have power.

I pressed the red button and bada-bing bada-bam, the power came back. Take that, Karma.

I found my phone and walked back to the kitchen. I restarted the washing machine and just as I sat down, the power went out again. A second round of vulgar curse words expelled from my mouth as I turned on the flashlight on my phone and reset the fuse again. Ukraine won that night; I was done trying to wash my clothes.

The following morning, I texted Elena, my colleague who had helped me solve the mouse problem. I explained that, although it sounded crazy, my washing machine was short-circuiting the electricity in my flat. Later that day, Elena, the two owners, and I stood cramped in my small kitchen. After the mice and cockroaches, a faulty washing machine brought us together yet again. We started the machine, and sure enough, the power went out. I shrugged my shoulders as they looked at me with the same look of astonishment I expressed the previous night.

They informed me that the best solution would be to check if there was a problem with the washing machine. I assumed that meant having someone come to my apartment to look at the machine in its place. It actually meant that two men would come to my apartment and remove my washing machine from the wall, carry it down two flights of stairs, and bring it to a repair shop.

I still had a pile of wet, dirty clothes sitting in my bathtub. Elena offered to wash them for me and I accepted her kind offer. I put everything in a bag for her and told her not to worry about air-drying the clothes at her place. I could do it here. I couldn't imagine my colleague hanging up my underwear to dry on her balcony when I had just met her three weeks ago.

Days turned into weeks, and by the first week of October, I still had a space in my kitchen where my washing machine once sat. I finally received a call from Elena that the machine was fixed. I was relieved that my colleague wouldn't have to wash my underwear anymore.

The machine was installed, and a few days later I pranced to my kitchen, happily and confidently putting my dirty clothes in the machine and turning it on.

Karma was a bitch, or Ukraine was playing a joke on me. The power went out.

I didn't curse this time. I laughed and I couldn't stop. The machine had been "fixed," and the same problem occurred. After two weeks, the problem was solved. A short circuit in the electricity had caused the power to go out. Even if I was gaining confidence in Ukraine, there was never a day without a surprise.

SLOW BEGINNING

The first few weeks in Zhytomyr didn't go how I had imagined them; neither good nor bad. I was prepared for difficulties, but I didn't anticipate the volume of daily surprises that I would have to deal with: managing vermin, furnishing an apartment, obtaining a working washing machine, and so forth. Despite things going slower than I had planned, I relied on riding the wave of positive energy that comes with living in a new place.

However, after living in Ukraine for about a month, I couldn't rely on that energy anymore. Since these everyday surprises took longer to solve than anticipated, I hadn't started my actual teaching job at the university until the end of September.

This wasn't my intention; I wanted to begin teaching earlier than this. A week prior, I had met with the dean on a Monday morning. I was ready to start teaching in whatever capacity they needed me. We agreed I would aid professors in topics including business, fashion, and geography, among others.

As the organized teacher I was trying to be, I sent out a Google sign-up sheet to all of the professors in my department, a total of ten women. On the sheet, I listed the days of the week and asked the professors to input their class times. My thought had been that I could attend the same professor's classes each week on the same day, at the same time. I wanted structure so I could schedule Ukrainian language lessons, workout classes, and travel time.

By the end of the week, I had zero inputs on my document. None of the professors had responded to my email. I checked my email for mistakes, but everything made sense to me.

After not receiving any responses, I decided to go to the university and ask the professors for their schedules in person. Little did I know I was about to be hit with the biggest surprise yet.

I walked into the teachers' room and caught one of the

professors on break. I asked her if she received my email about my schedule. I reiterated the intent of my email: I was trying to build a consistent schedule that allowed me to attend the same classes with the same professors each week.

She looked at me in confusion and said, "What do you mean you want to build a consistent schedule? Our classes change every week: the day, the time, and the room number."

I thought she was joking. "What do you *mean* the classes change every week?"

I never heard of a university that changed classes weekly, but it exists at a small university in Zhytomyr, Ukraine, the university I happened to be assigned.

I stood before the professor, speechless as I processed this new information. I wondered why the other professors and the dean had left out this detail. I thanked the professor and paced back to my apartment. I tried to understand why a university would create a system where one week you have class on Monday at 9:30 in the morning in Room 17 and the next week you have class at 3:20 in the afternoon on a Wednesday in Room 24. It seemed difficult for everyone involved: the dean, the professors, the students, and whoever organized the master schedule. I leaned against my apartment door, feeling the energy drain from me.

I had to contact ten professors individually the week before I actually started teaching. I asked them which classes I could come to on which day, at what time, and in what room. Multiply that by the number of weeks I would be teaching and you get a recipe for an organizational nightmare.

To me, there was no rhythm, no reason, and no pattern. But somehow I did it and I did it joyfully with collaboration from motivated professors, a coffee or snack waiting for me on my desk during break (thank you Natalie and Inna), and a little more energy than I thought I had.

REFRESHED

Before my first official class at the university, I wanted to get my nails done. One thing my family and friends know about me is that I never have naked nails. In Lviv, I had gotten my nails done with a friend, but that was a month ago by then.

The best way to find a good nail artist, eyebrow threader, or hairstylist in a new place is to ask people who have good nails, good eyebrows, and good hair. I had noticed Iryna always had a beautiful nail design each week at our Ukrainian lessons.

"Do you know where I could get my nails done?" I asked her during our next lesson.

She sent me the name and number of her nail artist. I scheduled an appointment with her and she sent me her address.

I arrived at the address, expecting to see a nail salon on the ground floor. Instead, I saw an eight-story, Soviet-style apartment. I walked up a few flights of stairs, found the correct apartment number, and nervously knocked on the door.

The woman who opened the door was a bubbly young blonde woman holding a baby girl in her arms. She welcomed me into her apartment with a smile. Her name was Irina.

I was skeptical at first. I had never gotten my nails done outside of a salon. However, Irina had transformed her balcony into a mini studio and had everything a typical salon would have: a heat lamp, colors, designs, and tools.

She put her daughter down for a nap and we began my manicure. I wasn't sure if we would have much to talk about, but our conversation shortly blossomed.

The baby started crying after thirty minutes. Irina took a break to breastfeed her; she was a businesswoman who could take care of her children and manage her career. I would continue to be amazed at Irina's flexibility, devotion to her children, and attention to detail in her work over the next six months.

She came back into the studio area, carrying Eva, the baby. Irina asked me if I wanted a coffee. As I replied yes, she handed me the baby and whisked away into the kitchen. The scene was unexpected, coming from an American culture where hospitality like this doesn't often exist, let alone being able to get your nails done in someone's apartment.

I was holding a stranger's baby while Irina made me a cup of coffee in the kitchen. It wasn't the nail salon experience that I imagined, but it was intimate and I enjoyed not just being a face in a busy salon.

Holding sweet Eva was heartwarming. She was only four months old. I couldn't remember the last time I had held a baby. Over the next few months, I would see Eva grow as my friendship with Irina also grew.

Irina came back into the room; she exchanged the coffee with me as I handed Eva to her gently. We sat on the couch in her living room as I drank my coffee, continuing our conversation. After two hours, my nails were fresh and perfectly manicured.

I was ready for my first class, made a new friend in Zhytomyr, and felt a little more at home.

INTO VIEW

It didn't become real until I stepped into my first classroom. The floors were tiled. Some tiles were broken, some moved beneath my feet as I walked, and others were missing altogether. The simple wooden desks, matching wooden chairs, and brightly-colored floor-length curtains dated the room. English grammar posters covered every inch of wall space.

I stood in front of a group of twenty university students. Our closeness in age struck me. I was twenty-three years old and they were nineteen or twenty. I was here to serve as their teacher, yet I had a feeling I would learn from them as much as they learned from me.

I didn't realize my hands were shaking until it was time to introduce myself and begin my lesson. I didn't know my students' English proficiency, the worst part of teaching a language to an unfamiliar class. *Would I be understood? Would my lesson be effective? Would they connect with me?*

My voice was introducing myself, but I couldn't hear it. In my mind, a tape was playing.

I was a business student studying marketing, finance, and accounting. I graduated with high marks. I participated in the summer business internships I was supposed to complete. I competed in and won entrepreneurship competitions, attended career fairs, and was recruited by corporate giants like Google.

I was doing what I was supposed to be doing, yet I was miserable, even depressed. The life that society and the business school were telling me was successful ate at my core. I was a walking hypocrite: caving in to the status quo of what others thought I should be doing, yet intimately believing success was something very different.

I was a traveler and writer. I studied literature in the Czech Republic, international economics in China, and fashion and photography in Italy. I traveled to thirty countries in Asia, Africa, and Europe. I connected with people around the world who shaped me and taught me different ways of life.

I was happy.

By the time I graduated from Villanova University in 2018, I had turned down several interviews and corporate opportunities. I was done living a life of hypocrisy defined by pressure, financial success, and never-ending expectations. My friend told me about a small summer camp in Ukraine where he taught English as a volunteer. I applied and soon purchased my flight ticket to Lviv, a city I had never heard of. My professors were shocked. I gave it all up to do what I knew would bring me joy, community, adventure, and fulfillment.

The bright curtains and English posters came back into view. Each student met my gaze. Their eyes spoke of their engagement, their excitement, and their curiosity. They asked questions and shared ideas about topics they wanted to learn more about. With each passing class, they brought me the joy, community, adventure, and fulfillment I had been seeking again; I prayed I brought them the same in return.

I was living a life aligned with the version of success I knew to be true for myself, the version I didn't have the courage to live previously. I walked out of my first class. My hands were no longer shaking, my breath was calm, and my heart was beating in a steady rhythm.

I was happy.

WINNING THE LOTTERY

Days of autumn had replaced the late summer nights. Fall was here; the sun was beginning to set earlier and the mornings were becoming colder. With a change of seasons, there was also a change in produce. At the market, new varieties of root vegetables, winter squashes, and apples of all types appeared every day.

I was organizing my notes and packing my bag in the teachers' room when Irena walked to my desk and asked, "Do you want to go to the market on Sunday to prepare your freezer for winter?"

A few weeks earlier, the owners bought a new refrigerator for my flat since the apartment didn't have one. I was expecting a small refrigerator, given the small size of the kitchen and others I had seen in my previous European flats.

My new refrigerator was just like the one my large family had in America, one with plenty of fridge space and an equally large freezer. I didn't mind the size, but I didn't need that much food space for just myself, especially if I would be spending a significant amount of time traveling. On the contrary, my colleagues applauded the owners for their thoughtful choice, further commenting that I would have plenty of room to store winter food.

I wanted to restock on fruits and veggies for the week ahead, so I told Irena I would be happy to join her at the market on Sunday.

She arrived at my flat a few days later. I held my wallet and a few tote bags as we exited my apartment. We met Valery and Vlada, her husband and daughter, who were parked and sitting inside their car. I assumed we were walking to the market across the street from my flat.

"Where are we going?" I asked, confused.

"We're going to the wholesale market to prepare for winter," she responded patiently.

All of my colleagues seemed to understand what it meant to "prepare your freezer for winter" and why the size of my freezer was a blessing; I didn't have the same understanding. The extent of my freezer usage in America and Ukraine thus far included a few extra bags of frozen veggies for lazy meals.

After driving through parts of Zhytomyr I hadn't yet seen, we arrived at a market that made the one near my flat look minuscule in comparison. There were vendors and trucks as far as I could see in each direction, each selling boxes of all kinds of fruits and vegetables.

I looked at the size of my tote bag and the size of the bags Irena brought.

"You can borrow my bags. What types of fruits and vegetables do you want for winter meals?" she asked.

Valery weaved ahead of us as we walked from stand to stand, trying to find the best bulk price for tomatoes, onions, potatoes, cabbages, peppers, and so on. I didn't have any words; I just observed his actions and the result of his successful bargaining. Box after box of produce was carried and piled into their car.

Irena explained that produce would be cheapest and most available in September and early October. They bought items in bulk now to save money and have access to these foods all year round. She would spend the next few days chopping, preparing, and storing the bulk produce. She would clean out the peppers, make sauce with the tomatoes, chop the onions, pickle the cucumbers, and store the potatoes in a cellar underground.

I came home with ten bunches of herbs, fifty potatoes, thirty tomatoes, thirty peppers, twenty-five carrots, and twenty onions, all for fifteen dollars. I had won the freezer lottery, but it came at a hefty price of preparation and adjusting to a new Ukrainian norm.

A PLANTED SEED

My morning espresso was brewing on the stove, filling the kitchen with a familiar heavenly aroma. I reached into the refrigerator for my soy milk, stepping carefully over bags of tomatoes, peppers, potatoes, and carrots.

I had rented an unfurnished apartment, purchased furniture and kitchenware, and now owned an entire kitchen's worth of food for the winter, all of which needed to be prepped for storage.

When I taught English in Ukraine in the summers of 2018 and 2019, my friends and I used to joke that every one day in Ukraine was equivalent to three days. With that logic, I would spend the next week (what felt like twenty-one days) cleaning, drying, peeling, chopping, blanching, and freezing everything I purchased.

I was fascinated by the tradition of preparing food for winter, a tradition that has been widely lost in the Western world. While there are individuals who have preserved this tradition in the United States and in other Western countries, the average American shops at supermarkets and buys what is needed regardless of the season. In the United States, we prioritize work, productivity, and convenience, and thus, we have a culture of packaged and fast food. To purchase seasonal, organic produce from local farmers in the United States is to often go above and beyond: research what types of food are in season, find local farm stands or grow the food yourself, spend a little extra time, and pay a little extra money.

We buy jarred pickles any time of the year. Ukrainians make pickles at the end of summer when cucumbers are harvested and enjoy them throughout the winter.

We buy apples any time of the year. Ukrainians plant orchards and reap the benefits throughout the fall. They store fresh apples in cellars and dry others to eat throughout the year.

We buy berries any time of the year. Ukrainians harvest berries in the summer, many of which are frozen for tea in the winter.

We buy mushrooms any time of the year. Ukrainians forage mushrooms and dry them for soups and dishes in the cold months.

My hands were red and blistered. My kitchen table was clean, the knives and chopping board were back in the cabinet, and the floor was swept. I filled my freezer with homemade tomato sauce, chopped peppers for curries, diced onions for stir fry, pesto for pasta dishes, and carrots for soups. Winning the freezer lottery wasn't something I asked for, but it planted the seeds of awareness and intentionality towards food, seasonality, and stewardship.

CONTRAST

Sickening: that's the only word I could think of to describe the contrast of my fully stocked freezer to the scene in front of me.

I was thankful to have finally settled into my apartment and teaching job. The surprises were frustrating, but they served as a reminder not to get too comfortable and to remain open to new solutions if something didn't work out at first. Would life have been easier had I gotten a comfortable, furnished apartment from the start? Absolutely, but I wouldn't have met the people I did, I wouldn't have explored the market and local stores, and I wouldn't have increased my confidence in my new home.

I wouldn't have seen the image that is as vivid in my mind as it was that day.

For the first few weeks, I didn't notice many people experiencing homelessness in Zhytomyr. Maybe I wasn't observant enough, or too focused on my own goals when I was out and about.

In what seemed like overnight, the large plot of grass behind my apartment had become home to five people. Not just a plot of grass, but the plot of grass next to the dumpster.

Naive, ignorant, privileged – call me what you want, but the scene was sickening. Five homeless people were sharing two wet, torn couches in an L-shape next to the dumpster. Pigeons sat on the armrests and bugs flew around.

I was throwing my trash away the first time I saw them. That's the part that sickened me the most; *I was throwing my trash away where these people were living.* Something felt so disgusting about disposing my garbage and walking back to the comfort of my apartment without doing anything to help them.

They lived there for weeks. I won't tell you what I did or didn't do. What we do in service of others stays in our hearts; what we don't do in service of others also stays in our hearts.

There was alcohol, there were drugs, and there was smoking.

One day after class, I turned the corner of my apartment building and was met with two men I recognized from the area near the dumpster. It was obvious both men were heavily intoxicated as they stumbled towards the back of the apartment complex. I paused as I watched them come to an unsteady halt against the door to my building. I noticed one of the men had an ax sticking out from the open zipper of his backpack.

Nobody else was near the apartment. I stood at a distance in the alleyway, considering if I should just wait for them to walk away. Before I had time to make a decision, a physical fight erupted between the two men. I think if there was ever a time I almost peed myself in fear, it was in that moment. As the men fought, I backed away slowly and stayed far away from my flat for hours until I thought it was safe to go back.

A few days later, the couches near the dumpster were gone and the people living there had vanished. I felt a selfish sense of safety, yet also a sense of grief for the people who called that one little space their home. I wondered every time thereafter if they found a new home, if they had a place to shower, or if someone extended a helping hand.

What we do in service of others stays in our hearts; what we don't do in service of others also stays in our hearts.

PAGES

An important part of my Fulbright experience in Ukraine was volunteering. My teaching job required me to work at the university for about twenty-five hours per week – a low number specifically designed to allow participants ample time to volunteer in the community, travel to different parts of the country, study Ukrainian or Russian languages, and explore Ukrainian culture.

Determining how and where to volunteer proved to be a challenge. There were countless projects and groups: student clubs, environmental outreach, homelessness support, Catholic nonprofits, and special education advocacy. The list went on and on.

I decided I would spend my time in two areas: student clubs and special education advocacy.

Within the first few weeks at the university, I developed and led three extracurricular clubs: English Speaking, Women in Leadership, and Business. Some of my greatest memories were engaging with students through these platforms.

What was equally important to me was special education advocacy. Before my Fulbright, I served as a teaching assistant to children with disabilities in a public school in New Jersey. I soon learned that, in Ukraine, special education doesn't exist in the same way. From what I understood, while disability advocacy is slowly progressing, there are limited government initiatives, adaptive school resources, and handicap infrastructure development, such as ramps or automatic doors, within cities and villages.

When I met with the dean to discuss my goals, one of them was to volunteer with disabled children, I was connected with a professor from a different department whose name was Natasha. I met her at the university one day in October. She introduced herself and opened up a box of chocolates for us at nine o'clock in the morning. I liked her already.

I learned that she started an English course for disabled children in Zhytomyr: some physically disabled, some with hearing problems, some with autism, some with learning disabilities. The students she worked with didn't have the same opportunity to learn English at school as the other children. What she was doing each week with them was the work of an incredible teacher.

For an hour on Mondays and Wednesdays, she taught English to a group of about ten children. I stayed in the background, getting to know the children slowly, helping pass out worksheets, and pronouncing a few words here and there.

To witness these children learning another language gave me chills each week. When I was frustrated with learning the Ukrainian language, my mind always returned to them.

After class one evening, Natasha invited me to her apartment for dinner. We were shocked to find out we only lived one block away from one another. She could practically see my apartment from her building.

I entered her flat, excited to meet a new face: Nadia, Natasha's daughter. Nadia had cerebral palsy. Natasha told me that she never assumed Nadia couldn't do something that other children could. She did the opposite; she encouraged her to try everything. The result was a young woman that radiated humility, grace, intelligence, and love.

It is difficult to describe what it was like to be in Nadia's presence. She told me stories and described the books she read in school. Not only did Nadia attend school, but she was in the gifted students' program. Nadia also played the piano for me, she knitted, and she showed me something I'll never forget: her book of prayers.

She opened the book to a page of smiley faces. There were easily 100 faces on the one page she showed me.

"What do the smiles represent?" I asked curiously.

"I draw a smiley face whenever I finish praying for someone," she responded.

She handed me the book gently. I flipped through the pages, mesmerized. She had filled page after page with thousands of smiley faces from top to bottom. My eyes filled with tears at the grace of this young woman who selflessly prayed for those around her. The world assumed she was the one who needed the most prayers, but Nadia showed me that prayers and love know no limit on this Earth.

LEAP OF FAITH

If I was going to accomplish my goal of running at least one half-marathon and one full marathon in Ukraine, I needed to make running a priority in my weekly schedule. Sunday morning trail runs were a good start; however, running six or seven miles once a week wasn't going to cut it.

I knew there were gyms in the city, but I preferred training on a terrain similar to that of a marathon race rather than a treadmill. I weighed my remaining options. The city streets were a viable option but were often crowded and filled with traffic. The trails winding through the forests surrounding the city were another promising option, but I didn't know them well enough to trek solo.

When I first moved into my apartment, Elena told me there was a field where I could play soccer nearby. I messaged her, asking for the name of the field so I could look it up.

I punched the name into Google Maps, put on my running clothes and shoes, and grabbed my headphones. The field was only a five-minute walk from my flat. I followed the arrow on the map, which led me to a modern stadium fit with a turf field, bleachers, and a well-kept track: a perfect place to run solo.

I stood by the six-foot metal fence surrounding the stadium. There was a swinging gate that was locked with a thick chain. I couldn't see another entrance, yet there were people inside who were running around the track.

I looked at the locked gate again and back to the people inside, wondering how to get in. I saw a construction worker nearby and gestured to him that I wanted to run like those on the track. He shrugged; it wasn't his problem that the gate was locked, and it wasn't his job to help someone who wanted to go inside. I could feel my frustration building. I used Google Translate to communicate that I was trying to run and didn't know how to enter the stadium. He shrugged again, but this time he pointed to a different area of the stadium and then to the locked gate.

He wrote on my phone, "Walk or jump."

I didn't want to walk ten minutes around the outside of the stadium just to be in a similar situation with a different fence. The more time I wasted trying to get inside, the less time I had to run before my first class.

I turned my back and walked to the locked gate in front of me. Without ample language skills, simple tasks became time-consuming, but that wasn't going to stop me from the goal I had set out to accomplish.

I landed on solid ground inside the stadium and looked back at the construction worker, who was chuckling. I don't think he ever saw a girl climb a six-foot fence, especially one who could've just walked to a different entrance.

I joined the other runners around the track, completed my training for the day, and happily walked home through the wide-open entrance on the opposite side of the track.

A UKRAINIAN AND RUSSIAN BEAT DOWN

Before my departure to Ukraine, I had never formally studied the languages of Ukrainian or Russian. I didn't even know the alphabet, greetings, or survival phrases. I didn't prepare beforehand under the pretense that more resources would be available when I arrived. This would become my biggest downfall – and my biggest accomplishment.

Orientation was over, and the comfort of being surrounded by my Fulbright colleagues was gone with it. I was alone in a new city where I didn't speak the language.

Four weeks later, I sat on my couch with my third cup of coffee in hand. I was mentally drained. My body felt like a ton of bricks had landed on it. I admired my furnished, one-bedroom apartment. I successfully bought a bed, rug, kitchenware, bedding, décor, household supplies, and everything else an apartment would need. I did it solo, and I did it without knowing either Ukrainian or Russian.

My shoulders slumped as my excitement began to wear off.

How was I going to do this for another eight months?

I spent my time in Ukraine without a firm knowledge of either language. During that period, I often felt beat down as everyday tasks became increasingly difficult. I tried to study, but excuse or not, another hurdle would appear. I should have felt motivated by these obstacles, but instead, I felt defeated with each one. When a grandma sat next to me on the bus and started speaking, I was frustrated I couldn't communicate effectively. When I hung out with my Fulbright friends who had studied either language in college, I felt embarrassed that I couldn't keep up. When I took an overnight train and couldn't understand what the conductor was saying to me, I felt small as my lack of understanding was revealed to the entire cabin. Not studying the languages before my arrival and consistently during my experience was my own repeating nemesis.

During those moments of self-defeat, I had one thing that reminded me to keep moving forward: my apartment. Imagine yourself in this situation. You have an empty apartment, no plates to eat off of or a bed to sleep on. You're living in a foreign city where you don't speak the languages. Everything is written in Cyrillic, so you can't even try to guess what the words mean. You don't have access to a big-box store or online retailer, so you have to go to mom-and-pop shops that each sell one type of product. You don't have a car. You're by yourself.

Ready, set, go.

I loved that accomplishment in my little bubble of the world, but when I return to Ukraine next time, I have a bigger goal. I'm going back with a deeper knowledge of Ukrainian and Russian languages, and I won't allow myself to give up. And while I'm at it, maybe I'll rent an apartment that's already furnished.

A CHANGE OF SEASONS

I had been living in Zhytomyr for a little over one month. I hadn't traveled anywhere new. I don't recall speaking to my family on the phone often, or my friends from home. I didn't reach out to my Fulbright cohort other than a few messages asking, "How are you?" or "How is your new city?" I was open to Zhytomyr but closed off from those around me.

When I look back on that first month, I smile at the joys of discovery and the fullness that came with it. I was discovering a new city that would be my home for nine months, even if I didn't know the language or was met with frustrating surprises. I was getting lost on the poorly paved streets between my apartment and the university. I was meeting eager students and learning how best to do the job I was there to do. I was breathing the newness of life in a foreign country.

I recall those moments of joy and independence so vividly only because I'm looking in hindsight. In truth, I was hurting in the still moments.

I was lost, my mind wandering in the thoughts of which parts of myself I wanted to leave behind and which parts I wanted to foster.

I was lonely, fearful of letting new people into my life yet too stubborn to confide in those whose support was just a phone call away.

I was distrusting, my heart still healing from the cracks of a broken relationship with someone who was in the same country I was now living in.

I looked at my hand and twisted the metal band of empty promises around my left finger. *Which parts of myself did I want to leave behind and which parts did I want to move forward with?*

I packed my bags and sat on an outdated bus in transit to Kyiv. The dirt roads laden with gravel and potholes soon turned into a modern, paved highway. I saw the familiar skyscrapers I had seen during orientation. The energy of the hustling and bustling city appearing before me contrasted with the quieter life I was living in Zhytomyr.

I arrived at the hotel where I would be attending a week-long conference from October 6–11; it was the same hotel we had stayed in a few weeks prior during orientation. I stood at the check-in desk and began to see familiar Fulbright faces fill the lobby. I talked to a few friends, briefly catching each other up on the first month in our host cities. The same conversations continued into dinner. We got more comfortable with each other, laughed at one another's stories, eager to listen to the next one, and found contentment in being with each other again. I realized I was laughing more than I had in weeks. As the evening turned into night, I let out a deep sigh of relief that I didn't know I had been holding in.

We began the next morning with a tour of Kyiv. The October morning was crisp and the leaves had begun to turn colors. We walked along a descending path, stopping at a view atop the open square of Maidan. The tour guide's voice faded into the background as my eyes looked to the people around me, people who had begun to bring me a sense of fullness again. I looked down at the colorful leaves painted beneath my feet. Fall was here, and with it a change of seasons, a change that held a part of me that I could finally let go of.

FOOL ME ONCE, SHAME ON YOU

One day before arriving at the hotel for our conference, I met my two Fulbright friends in Kyiv: Sydney and Amelia. Our idea had been to spend an extra day exploring the city and seeing new sites, something we didn't have time to do during our busy orientation week a month before, and something we knew we wouldn't have time to do during our conference either.

We met at a church near the city center where Sydney was playing the bells. I had missed her performance since my bus from Zhytomyr arrived two hours after I anticipated, an occurrence I later learned to plan for. Sydney and Amelia climbed down from the steep bell tower, meeting me with open arms and smiles.

We couldn't get the words out fast enough when my friend interrupted our conversation, saying, "Our host just responded. We're meeting her in one hour at this restaurant."

She typed in the address on Google Maps. It was already getting dark, and we needed to find our way there. I faced both of them with trepidation, "Are we sure about this?"

One hour later, we nervously sat in the restaurant sharing

a piece of chocolate cake and waiting for our host. Even though we were anxious, we each had expressed reasons why we wanted to do this: 1) we didn't want to pay for a hostel, 2) we didn't want to repeat the same generic hostel experience each of us had in many different cities on our previous travels, and 3) we wanted to meet locals in a meaningful way. Couchsurfing checked all three of those boxes.

Two weeks before, we made profiles on a site called Couchsurf. The premise of the platform is to connect travelers with locals willing to host them. In your profile, you write the skills you can teach or the stories you can share with the host in exchange for a couch or a place to sleep. Ideally, hosts would also write what they could teach you or that they could show you their city from a local's perspective. The best part of the platform is that it's completely free. The worst part is that you don't know if someone's profile is who they really are.

I tried to eat a bite of cake, but I couldn't stomach it. *Couchsurfing seemed like a win-win, but why did I have this mounting fear in my stomach that our host wasn't who she said she was?*

It was too late to worry as my friend stood up and said, "Hi, my name is Sydney, and these are my two friends: Amelia and Kat."

We felt like a part of their family, if only for a short period. We met their children. We shared wine and cake that I could stomach this time. We practiced Ukrainian and spoke Italian, drank espresso and tea, and wandered around their village just outside of Kyiv. We told stories and took pictures. They trusted three American strangers, and we trusted them. Our stay was up, but in my head, it wasn't. The trust we shared would stay with me. Society taught me to be afraid of strangers, to be distrusting, and expect the worst.

That's society's fear, not mine.

WORTH THE PAIN

Outside of my day-to-day job at the university, running in Zhytomyr was one of the most meaningful ways I connected with my host city. It kept me grounded and reminded me that I had community and that there were opportunities for exploration in my backyard. It's something I wish I could have done more of.

Sometimes our bodies don't align with our minds. My mind wanted to participate in trail runs every Sunday morning, but my knees were screaming a different narrative. After my first trail run of seven miles, I felt the same pain I had experienced months prior. I ignored it and kept running, wanting to trick my mind that connecting with the community outweighed my pain.

I returned from our week-long conference in Kyiv, followed by a weekend trip to Rome, where I was reunited with my brother and a few friends. It was a Sunday morning in mid-October, and I was back to my running routine in Zhytomyr. The running group and I gathered at our usual meeting point in the park. We started jogging across the pedestrian bridge, over the river, and into the forest. With each step, my knees ached in pain.

I trailed at the back of the group. One runner, who always welcomed me with a smile, saw I was slowing down. His name was Viktor. He was in his fifties and made running look effortless. On the first day I met him, he brought a medal from his last race: an ultramarathon of fifty miles. If he could run fifty miles, then I could keep pushing through the pain.

He slowed his pace to meet mine. I smiled, my way of thanking him for staying back with me when I knew he could run faster and longer without me. He asked if I wanted to run a marathon in Ukraine. My face lit up. I wanted to answer yes, but the sharp pain in my knees knew the real answer. I told him that I wanted to run, but I didn't want to make my injury worse.

Over the next six miles, he never left my side. First, we only spoke about things in common: our running journeys, past injuries, and life in Zhytomyr. As the miles increased, our conversations became more personal. I began to forget about the pain as his stories enraptured me. He explained what his life was like during the beginning of the war in Ukraine and how he served as a commander on the frontline. He spoke of the difficult moments when he wouldn't call his wife or family for weeks because he didn't want them to be scared of the bombs and gunshots going off in the background. He said that life was never the same after witnessing what he saw in the East; he knew what mattered in his life and what didn't.

Viktor was full of wisdom and courage that went beyond ultra-running. Hearing his life story showed me a different side to the faces I encountered in Zhytomyr. When I committed to moving to Ukraine, I yearned to see life beyond that of an American just exploring the surface of a foreign city. I wanted to hear stories like Viktor's, stories of strength and perseverance overcoming that of pain and suffering – stories of humanity.

My knees throbbed in pain as we reached the top of the hill at the park where we had begun our sunrise run. He high-fived me, as was the custom with each member of the group, and gave me one last piece of advice: "Don't ever run with pain again."

He was right, but after a run like that, I wasn't sure I could ever stop.

STARTING POINT

The longer I stayed in Zhytomyr, the more my travel bug grew. During our orientation in September, our program director suggested that we stay in our host cities for a few weeks to get settled and become familiar with our universities and surroundings. Aside from our mandatory conference and a family weekend trip to Rome, and despite my mounting travel bug, I heeded her advice and stayed in Zhytomyr.

I had come to a place of confidence in my daily routine in Zhytomyr: my teaching "schedule," exploration, fitness timeline, and community engagement. However, being at the conference in Kyiv showed me that I needed to amend one thing in my schedule: I needed to make time for friends and fun.

I knew a place where I would find both friends and fun: Lviv.

Even though I had spent ten days in Lviv at the end of August, it felt like a lot of time had passed. So much had happened in my daily life in Zhytomyr since then. I was content in my Zhytomyr home, but it was time to see my friends. I booked my first solo coach bus for Friday, October 18, direct from Zhytomyr to Lviv. I would stay in Lviv for the weekend and return by the start of class on Monday.

I had taken local marshrutkas from Zhytomyr to Kyiv. There was a bus station one block from my apartment where buses to Kyiv left frequently. They were easy to find and navigate (except for the schedule).

This bus would be different. It was departing from the main bus station in Zhytomyr, where hundreds of buses come in and out every hour: marshrutkas, local buses, coach buses, and even international buses. I didn't think it could be that hard to find my bus to Lviv. I was very wrong.

I was always learning during my time in Ukraine. There were too many challenges to not learn something new, even if you didn't want to. I learned that day that bus travel in Ukraine is not for the faint of heart. Unless you are a local, have a strong grasp of Ukrainian or Russian languages, or organize a tour meant for foreigners, you will be lost in a maze of confusion, people, and buses.

I called Irena as the clock neared my departure time to ask her if there was a trick to finding my bus. I was so excited to see my camp friends in Lviv and meet a few Fulbright friends who were also visiting Lviv that weekend. That wouldn't happen if I couldn't find my bus.

Just as I was admitting defeat to Irena, a bus pulled in that read "Львів." It was my bus. I spent six hours on the winding and bumpy path to Lviv, to the place where my journey with Ukraine began.

PERMISSION

A big question mark that loomed overhead during my first few weeks in Ukraine was obtaining my legal residence permit. Since I decided to arrive in Ukraine ten days earlier than the start of our orientation, my visa expired ten days earlier than my colleagues. Before my arrival, I received a ninety-day visa from the Ukrainian Consulate in New York City. The start day was August 26. It would end on November 24.

In order to legally stay in Ukraine, I had to obtain a residence permit by the end date of my visa. I was warned that the process could take months, was often a bureaucratic nightmare, and may even arrive after the expiration of my visa. Arriving ten days early didn't seem like a big difference to me, but apparently it was. To obtain the permit, I needed to provide my residing address, passport copies, official photos, and a letter of intent from my university. I also needed to secure Ukrainian health insurance and fill out endless paperwork. Every day, it seemed like I needed to produce another signature, for what, I don't know.

For that reason, I stayed in Zhytomyr from the end of October through the first two weeks of November. My life was simple and predictable: I taught my classes, ran with the club, attended my fitness and Ukrainian language classes, and planned meetings for extracurricular clubs. I needed to be on call, as the time was ticking towards the expiration of my visa. I was getting nervous; I would be traveling internationally on November 22. Without a permit in my hand, I couldn't leave or reenter the country.

On November 15, Irena called me after weeks of diligently working on my paperwork, another reason I was incredibly thankful for her. She informed me that my residence permit was ready to be picked up.

After nearly three months since the day I arrived in Ukraine, I held my residence permit in hand, beaming with joy that the paperwork and the anxious waiting period were over. The card was supposed to be valid until my departure: June 2020. Much to my surprise, the Ukrainian government granted me a residence card with permission to live in the country until the year 2023.

Four years. I could live in Ukraine for four years. The number was shocking to me, and the fact that I was arbitrarily gifted such a long extension. I was the first of my colleagues to receive my residence permit since I was the first of the cohort to arrive in Ukraine. Thank you to my Ukrainian summer romance for pushing me to return to Ukraine early.

I spent the day dreaming about all of the possibilities of what I could do in a foreign country for four years: I could volunteer, write, and continue teaching. Maybe I could use Ukraine as my base point and become a full-time travel blogger. The possibilities were endless.

The possibilities were endless. It was time for me to get on the road.

GONE WRONG

After finally obtaining my residence permit and after taking a few local trips, I was getting more comfortable with the idea of traveling to new places in Ukraine. I had experience traveling in the western part of the country. I wanted to see someplace different; I wanted to go someplace east.

I booked a one-way express train ticket to my destination: Kramatorsk. It was a six-hour train ride, leaving on Saturday, November 16 at 6:30 in the morning from the main station in Kyiv. Zhytomyr was a two-hour bus ride from Kyiv, which meant I had to arrive and stay in the capital the night before.

A week before my trip, I messaged a Fulbright colleague who was placed in Kyiv and asked her if I could spend the night at her apartment. She had an extra bed for guests and told me to call her when I arrived that Friday.

I arrived in Kyiv as planned and messaged her when I was on my way to her flat. By the time I arrived, it was almost nine o'clock in the evening. My message was left unanswered, so I decided to call her. There was no response.

I waited for twenty minutes outside a nearby grocery store, wondering if she lost track of time or maybe had fallen asleep. My phone was losing battery quickly. After thirty minutes, my screen lit up. It was my friend calling.

"I'm so sorry! I'm in another city for the weekend. I got the dates mixed up!" she apologized.

There was nothing I could do; it was an honest mistake. I had ten percent battery left on my phone and was alone in a neighborhood of Kyiv I didn't know well. I went inside the safety of the grocery store and looked up hostels. I booked the first one that had decent reviews and was located between where I was standing and the train station.

I walked thirty minutes to the hostel, where I had reserved a bed in a female-only dorm. My friend called me again to make sure I had found a place to sleep. She felt terrible for leaving me hanging and had tried to call her roommates to open the apartment, but they were also out of town. She had even called another Fulbrighter, who responded just after I had already booked a hostel. I texted and assured her that it wasn't a problem; I appreciated her willingness to help, but I was okay and had a place to sleep.

As my phone battery decreased, my nerves heightened. If my phone died, then I'd be stranded, and I'd be stranded at night. I walked down an alleyway, relieved to find my hostel. I arrived close to eleven o'clock, cringing at the thought that I would have to wake up in less than six hours for my train.

The receptionist welcomed me and informed me that there was only one other woman in my room. She was from America; we had something in common.

He knocked and opened the door with her permission. We were both hit by a wall of incense and smoke. We may have both been American, but we surely had different thoughts on hostel etiquette.

I waited in the common room while the room aired out, judging her with what little energy I had left. After thirty minutes, my fatigue overtook my pettiness and I reentered the room.

The smell of incense still lingered. She apologized for the smell, saying she thought there weren't other guests staying in the dorm. I knew there were nights when I mistakenly thought I had a hostel dorm to myself too, so I let it go. I didn't have any intention of continuing the conversation; I was exhausted from my night of unexpected adventure. I unpacked my toiletries and pajamas, knowing the time between now and my wake-up call was growing slimmer by the minute.

Two hours later, I was still sitting on my bed with my toothbrush and pajamas in hand. One moment I was planning on staying at a friend's place, the next moment I was stranded, and the following I was considering sleeping in the hostel common room. Now it was well past one o'clock in the morning and I was talking to a backpacker about life and the beauty of slow travel. Maybe everything I thought went wrong that night went right. What was wrong was my perspective and quickness to judge. I rested my head on the pillow, thankful that I had a six-hour train ride to catch up on sleep.

JOURNEY TO THE EAST

Are you sure it's safe to go there? Those heavy words rang in my ears as I boarded my first Ukrainian train, an express train heading 430 miles to the East of Ukraine. I was told this part of the country was different, that it seemed like it wasn't part of the same country I had been living in for three months. The wheels of the train began rolling. I thought I would be able to catch up on sleep, but I didn't anticipate the nerves that began to settle in my stomach. In less than a few hours, I would be arriving in a formerly occupied city called Kramatorsk, a city that sits about sixty miles from the frontline of the war between Russia and Ukraine.

As the train continued eastward, I felt a strong sense of uneasiness. There was an unspoken heaviness in the air. Recognizable tourists had exited the train long before. As I looked around, I noticed those who remained. I studied the deep creases on the faces of older people, wrinkles that aged them faster than what time allowed. I looked at the professionals, wondering who they would be meeting when we arrived. I looked at the mothers whose eyes held the depths of responsibility and stress. I looked at the young people and wondered if they had been displaced by the war. *Were the people sitting around me holding onto a similar story like Viktor's, my running friend?* I remained unsettled, but I knew that visiting this city was something I wanted to do.

We soon arrived at the train station. I exited the wagon and was relieved to meet my Fulbright friend, Grayson. He smiled and welcomed me with open arms. After we dropped my bags off at his dorm, we began exploring.

Slowly, curiosity replaced my uneasiness. Over the next two days, we visited the main square and the local market, drank coffee and tea, shared meals, talked with locals, and wandered around the city without an agenda. I enjoyed the simplicity of the weekend as my days in Zhytomyr had become filled with responsibilities and classes and were often accompanied by the self-imposed feeling of always needing to do more. In Kramatorsk, that feeling disappeared. Maybe it was because I was reunited with an American. Maybe it was because I didn't have classes. Or maybe it was because I surrendered to what being present can do to you if you let go of your plan.

I expected the city to be different, but not in the way it turned out. In those moments of simplicity, sharing tea and chocolate each night with my friend and laughing about how much Ukraine had changed us, I didn't remember where I was. I didn't think about the city's past. I didn't think about that feeling of uneasiness when I first arrived. I didn't think about it, yet it was impossible to forget. That joy would always be juxtaposed with the harsh reality of the war next door. It would be juxtaposed with the war-torn stories we heard from those affected. It would be juxtaposed with the silence that filled the streets each night, reminiscent of a time when the city once had a curfew. That sense of joy and harshness paralleled the ebb and flow of life we all experience, in any place in the world, in Ukraine, and in Kramatorsk.

MAY WE NEVER MEET AGAIN

During my previous travels to Ukraine in the summers of 2018 and 2019, I had stayed in the same village for the duration of my trips, except when visiting Lviv on the weekends. I had never taken Ukrainian public transportation. I navigated buses and trains in other countries, but the thought of figuring out public transportation with signs in Cyrillic spooked me.

By the end of my weekend in Kramatorsk, I had successfully taken one coach bus to Lviv, a few marshrutkas to the capital of Kyiv, and an express train to the East. On my way to Kramatorsk, I chose an express train for my first leg of the trip but didn't like the timing or cost of the express train on the way back. The remaining option was to take my first overnight train.

Here's how Ukrainian overnight trains work. There are three classes:

- **Sleeping wagon (first class):** a closed compartment with two single beds; most expensive option

- **Coupe (second class):** a closed compartment with four beds (two bunks); more expensive than third class, but not as much as first class

- **Platzkart (third class):** an open wagon where passengers sleep on bunk beds in a carriage with about sixty other people; cheapest option

I asked friends and colleagues which option was best and

received mixed reviews. Some preferred the privacy of second class but said the compartment gets stuffy and hot since it's closed off. Some preferred the bottom bunk in third class because it was cheaper and more spacious. Others liked the top bunk with its own space above everyone else.

I stared at the train website. First class was out of the picture since it was too expensive for my budget travels. Second class was a good option, but I decided I wouldn't be comfortable if I was in a compartment with three other men. Third class was the winner: it was cheaper and roomier. Now came the task of choosing the top or bottom bunk. I loved sleeping on the top bunk as a child, so I figured that was the best option.

I was three hours into my first twelve-hour overnight train. It was one o'clock in the morning. I laid on the top bunk staring at the luggage rack one foot above my head. I wanted to sit up, but I couldn't. Nausea kept me awake as the train swayed back and forth. I cursed the motion sickness that had followed me into my twenties. I needed to get some fresh air but didn't know how to get down without disturbing the passenger below me.

I closed my eyes, hoping the sound of the train would lull me to sleep, but another wave of nausea hit me. I finally jumped down and spent the next three hours in the corridor between the two wagons, the only place with access to outside air, which also happened to be next to the bathroom.

The mindless hours passed. It was four o'clock in the morning. I gave myself a pep talk and made my way back to my top bunk.

We finally arrived, and I stepped onto the train platform,

feeling rejuvenated to be on solid ground. I looked back at the wagon where I had spent the last twelve hours. It was cheap, but I'd be damned if I'd ever sleep on a top bunk again. You can take the girl off the top bunk, but you can't take the budget traveler out of the girl.

A BIG VILLAGE

Returning from the East felt light. It was a relief to be far away from the war. I spent the week thinking about Kramatorsk, wondering what it would have been like if I was placed there instead of Zhytomyr.

When I first found out about my placement in Zhytomyr, I was neither enthusiastic nor upset. I was praying to be placed in Western Ukraine, near Lviv, in hopes of being close to my Ukrainian friends from the summer camps I taught at. To be honest, I had never heard of Zhytomyr. When I Googled the city back in May, I couldn't find much information. I couldn't be upset about a place I didn't know anything about.

At our orientation in Kyiv, my feelings shifted as more and more locals snickered and joked when I told them where I was placed.

"Oh, Zhytomyr. I'm sorry. At least you're close to Kyiv."

"Oh, Zhytomyr. It's so small."

"Oh, Zhytomyr. There's not much to do there."

I couldn't describe on the surface what there was to do in Zhytomyr, but there was always something. Those people weren't wrong; the city was close to Kyiv, it was small (about 260,000 people), and there wasn't much listed on travel websites like TripAdvisor. Yet, I was always busy, always looking forward to a class or a get-together, trying new cafes, and meeting new people.

Sure, some cities are more challenging to live in than others. Some cities may be too small or too large. Some cities may not be the number one travel destination. But Zhytomyr wasn't any of that to me; it was a city to live in, to grow in, and to see a different way of living, if only for a short period.

I did what I did for that reason. I put myself out there: taking yoga classes, volunteering with disabled children, going to Mass every Sunday, taking fitness classes with Iryna, shopping locally, getting dinner with Irena and her family, and meeting with students outside of class. It was uncomfortable for me to do these things at times, but the result was always worth the discomfort, even on that Wednesday night.

After a few weeks of participating in the running club, my knee pain was as bad as the pain of my original injury, IT band inflammation. I couldn't run anymore and I couldn't participate in the fitness classes I pre-purchased each month. I had gone to an American clinic in Kyiv and got an MRI. I had exacerbated my original injury, adding cartilage damage to each knee.

I could bear doing yoga once a week; at least *all* my classes wouldn't go to waste. There was only one yoga class offered each week at a time I could attend: Wednesday evening.

I changed into my yoga leggings and a tank top, bundled up, and headed to the studio, about a fifteen-minute walk. I loved working out with Iryna and running with the club, but sometimes it was nice to work out in a class where no one knew me.

I thought that night would be one of those nights where I could just escape. On my way to the studio, I walked past the cafe where Iryna and I often met after classes for Ukrainian language tutoring sessions. I saw a group of three girls. Not just a group of girls, my students. I smiled, surprised to see them outside of class. We chatted and I told them that I would love to meet for coffee soon, but I had a yoga class that was about to start.

"So do we," they answered in unison.

We looked at each other as I asked them, "Where is your class?"

They pointed to the building next to the cafe. We took a yoga class together that night. That was the epitome of Zhytomyr that I couldn't describe to others. Zhytomyr, was, as locals called it, "a big village."

A TIME FOR THANKS

I was escaping the guilt trip I had encountered as the days crept closer to the holidays. It was November 27, another cloudy day. The thought of not being home for Thanksgiving was gnawing at me like the cold air around me. I used some of my "out-of-country" days, allotted days where I was allowed to leave Ukraine, and traveled through Slovakia, the Czech Republic, and Austria from November 22–27. I met old travel friends dotted along the way, friends who I had met in different countries and were just like me, ready for the next adventure.

Five days were up as quickly as they had come. I had masked my guilt with traveling and let my new memories sweep me back into my reality in Ukraine. I landed at the airport in Kyiv and was blindsided with a different wave of emotion: culture shock.

How could I experience culture shock when I was only gone for a week?

Just as quickly as I felt the shock, someone else noticed too. I was taken out of my trance as I looked up to a car that had pulled up to the passenger drop-off area. The black car shifted into park as the back window rolled down. A man's words pierced my ears, "You're going to hate your life here."

In an instant, the car was gone.

My feet felt frozen to the ground. His words echoed as I tried to process why he said what he did.

My phone buzzed; my Uber arrived.

I looked up. The same black car was parked in front of me again. It was my Uber.

I canceled the Uber and started walking, erasing his words with each step. It's a funny thing when you're in a foreign country and something like that happens. A small comment can change the course of your day or how you perceive the place you're in. I don't know why the driver said what he said, but I reminded myself that, while experiencing culture shock was difficult, I had a community here, I had a place to live, and I had the joy of adventure even through the ups and downs. Plus, I had friends waiting for me just a drive away.

I had friends waiting for me just a drive away. I was so caught up that I forgot my Fulbright friends had arrived from their host cities to celebrate Thanksgiving. I looked at my messages for the first time since I landed, reading texts I missed. We were meeting for dinner in an hour.

I took a bus and then hopped on the metro. I was fighting rush hour and arrived ten minutes late. As I walked into the restaurant, I asked the hostess, "Americans?"

She offered me a nod and gestured for me to follow her. I turned a corner and saw a stack of backpacks near the coat rack. I hadn't noticed the tension I felt in my shoulders from carrying my backpack all week. I added mine to the pile and turned to meet my friends. With one look, I let go of the holiday guilt, culture shock, and everything I had felt in the last hour. I had friends just a drive away, and that was something I couldn't be more thankful for.

FOOL ME TWICE, SHAME ON ME

I yearned to travel in a newer way, in a more conscious state that allowed me to live outside the predictability of the life I left behind. Over the last few years, I have traveled to thirty other countries, each with unique adventures and stories. I had seen so many different places, but I couldn't ignore the feeling that I was replacing my old routine with a new life that had become just as predictable. Pick a new city, look up a hostel with reviews above eight on a ten-point scale, reserve a bed in a female-only dorm, make sure the hostel offers guided tours and is located in the city center. Or in other words, wander far, but not too far, stay inside your comfort zone, and repeat how society tells you how to travel.

Society taught me how to travel, and I don't know how it happened. Maybe it happened before my first move abroad when I was nineteen. Maybe it happened during my first international solo trip. Maybe it happened when I moved to a "developing" country. Each time, I was congratulated for leaping, but... There was always a *but*. Every well-wish was contrasted with a warning: "Be careful," "It's not safe there," and "Don't travel as a solo female."

As I paved my way through each country, often solo, I pushed others' concerns out of my mind. I wanted to believe the world wasn't a big, scary place. If I believed this, then why had I fallen into a routine of comfort, a routine where I could've been at any hostel in any part of the world and wouldn't have noticed any difference?

The metal gate closed behind us. We were in a village outside of Kyiv. The knot that had twisted itself in my stomach at dinner doubled. My friend shot me a look that told me she was feeling the same. She whispered, "This is the part where we get kidnapped."

The lights were off and we didn't know what time it was. The three of us were sharing a pull-out couch in a stranger's house, telling stories about our previous travels that had led us each to this moment.

As we were quietly chatting, I replayed what went through my mind hours before. When the host closed the gate, I felt like we entered a real-life horror film. I could picture the news headline the next day saying: *Three American Females Kidnapped while Couchsurfing*.

Sydney paused in the middle of our conversation and asked in seriousness, "Why does society believe that bad things will happen if we trust strangers? What if we believed that strangers were good people who wanted to help?"

Her words sat with me as we reflected on our first Couchsurfing experience on that October night. I wanted to believe in the goodness of strangers, but society still held a grip on me.

Before Thanksgiving, I messaged the same two friends, saying, "I think we should Couchsurf again." Maybe the first time we Couchsurfed was a fluke and our hosts were just nice people. I needed to try it again. I needed to trust strangers and find an answer to the questions my friend asked that night.

It was dark again as we found ourselves in the same situation in Kyiv. The three of us were walking on a dimly lit street on our way to meet our Couchsurfing host, a male host. I cursed myself as the same knot twisted in my stomach. For the second time, I couldn't push away the nagging fear that the worst was going to happen. As our host closed the door behind us, I whispered the same prayer I had weeks before, a prayer that I could trust the goodness of this stranger.

AN ANSWERED PRAYER

One of our caveats for Couchsurfing was that we would only stay with female hosts. Before Thanksgiving, I messaged a woman on the site who had a son and husband and hundreds of positive reviews written on her profile. If she welcomed strangers into her family and trusted them around her child, my friends and I could extend the same trust.

A week before we were supposed to arrive, I received a message from our host saying that she mixed up the dates and realized she would be in Thailand with her son during the time we were supposed to stay. I thought it sounded a little odd, but she assured us that her husband would be happy to welcome us and that we could still sleep there.

Three girls and one male host. It sounded like a scene that my mother would cringe at, swearing that I was crazy for putting myself in this situation. I promised her and my family I would travel safely, but I needed to learn to trust strangers. I decided to do this, and I needed to stand behind that decision.

We walked down the alley behind the apartment complex, agreeing we would only meet hosts during daylight if there was a next time we did this. I called our host and he came outside to meet us. We were met by a man with a friendly but uneasy smile.

My friend stood up to the plate again. "Hi, my name is Sydney, and these are my two friends: Amelia and Kat."

We followed him to his fourth-floor apartment. As the door closed behind us, I wondered if his wife was telling the truth. He was uncomfortable, pacing around the apartment as he showed us where we would be sleeping. We saw children's toys scattered on the floor, a validation that part of his wife's story was true; they had a child. My friends and I made eye contact at the same time. We could ease our worries.

We sat at his kitchen table as he nervously chopped vegetables with shaky hands and tried to make conversation. It was almost ten o'clock at night. We had already eaten, but we thought it would be rude to decline his homemade meal and go straight to bed. We asked him what he was preparing and if he needed any help chopping.

"Chilli paneer. It's a dish I learned how to make when I was in India," he said.

I had to stop my mouth from dropping open. A Ukrainian

man was making a spicy Indian dish for us. An aroma of spices I hadn't smelled in months filled the kitchen. I wasn't hungry, but there was no way I was passing up Indian food. Trying to find spicy food in Ukraine is like trying to find a needle in a haystack.

We ate together, our eyes and noses running from the spices, a sensation I happily welcomed. We talked about his travels to Asia, and he seemed comfortable for the first time since our arrival. He had lived and traveled around different Asian countries for months at a time, sometimes with his wife and son and sometimes solo. They had a deep interest in Asian culture, something that also surprised me and again affirmed his wife's story. He told us about his life before marriage and fatherhood, shocking us with stories of spending summers camping for weeks and canoeing hundreds of kilometers throughout the former Soviet Union.

Since it was nearing midnight, we thanked him for the conversation and delicious meal and he wished us a good night's sleep. We closed our bedroom door and climbed onto the pull-out couch. The three of us could only fit if we slept sideways.

Our host was no different than us; we were all travelers and humans seeking community, depth, and trust in strangers.

PUT IT ALL ON ME

After Couchsurfing the night before Thanksgiving, we stayed in a hostel for the remainder of our long weekend trip. Eight Fulbrighters would be staying together, an impossible feat to find a Couchsurfing host who could accommodate a group of our size.

With every group that wants to travel together, the responsibility of organizing and planning inevitably falls upon one or two people, and if it doesn't, nothing will get done. Somehow that job was relayed to me, and I was happy with it. If a task involves travel and planning, I'm all for it.

After traveling the way I had for the last few years, my standards were not the height of luxury. As I said, I was content sleeping in a hostel as long as it was clean and safe, situated in a good location, and had decent reviews. We needed a mixed dorm where we could book the entire room up front, and it had to be close to the Fulbright office and downtown Kyiv so we could easily commute to our events and meetings. We also wanted to keep the price low since we were paying for it out of pocket.

One part of the group wanted to stay in an Airbnb because it offered better amenities. However, as we had learned on our last trip together, an Airbnb usually only has one or two sets of keys. This turns into a logistical nightmare if eight people have eight different plans for the day. An Airbnb was off the table.

My hostel search continued. I found three hostels with decent reviews and could accommodate all of us for the dates we needed. One of them was less than a ten-minute walk to the Fulbright office and the main street in Kyiv and was only ten dollars per night. The other two also fit our criteria. I created a poll with the three options and submitted it to our group chat.

When I created the poll, I assumed that everyone would take the time to research each hostel and read the reviews, before giving their opinion. I don't know if that happened, but everyone said they agreed on the hostel closest to the Fulbright office: Hostel Olive.

I booked an eight-person room for three nights. It was thirty dollars per person for the long weekend. Everyone reimbursed me and all seemed well until the week before we were supposed to arrive. We received an email from our program director asking us to submit a receipt so we could be reimbursed for our accommodations. This email was a surprise to us as we had previously been told that we had to pay for our own stays.

We would not have chosen to sleep in an eight-person budget dorm room if we knew that we would be reimbursed. I wrote to the group, "Should we change our reservation and find something with separate rooms and better facilities?"

The majority voted that we should just stick with what we already decided. Let the record hold that I provided two opportunities for the group to vote.

We arrived at Hostel Olive on Thanksgiving morning, November 28. My friends and I were shocked. It was not the same hostel we saw online. There were no locks on the doors. The lockers were so small that they couldn't even fit a backpack. The kitchen was dirty. There were random rugs and storage under the bunk beds in our room.

Everyone turned to me, and suddenly I was the person single-handedly responsible for the hostel's shortcomings. Even if my friends were joking, the blame was on me. I tried to defend myself and then shrugged. I was happy with a bed to sleep on.

Long live Hostel Olive. You win some, you lose some.

UNDER PRESSURE

During our fall conference in Kyiv, my Fulbright friend Grayson and I took a hot yoga class. It was fun to be with another American, and the class was easier to follow than my usual fitness classes in Zhytomyr.

It was the end of November and we were all back in Kyiv again. I asked Grayson if he wanted to take another hot yoga class, to keep our little tradition up. Our other friend Amelia was also interested. We signed up for a morning yoga class on Thanksgiving Day.

Our Couchsurfing host was located on the outskirts of Kyiv, a thirty-five-minute drive to the city center. It was rush hour, and our drive turned into one hour.

We missed our yoga class. I was bummed and angry at myself for not leaving earlier. The small consistencies gave me something to look forward to, especially on a holiday that looked a lot different this year.

Thankfully, Sydney, who was also in the car with us, found another yoga class on the other side of the city. Thanksgiving Day got a little brighter.

We arrived well in advance and took our spots in the studio. As with my first fitness class in Zhytomyr, it was evident that we were not locals. The teacher asked us if we spoke Russian or Ukrainian. Grayson took one for the team and did all the talking. The studio was filled with fifteen other people, all of whom were dead silent when Grayson was speaking.

For the next hour and a half, we followed the instructor and sweat profusely. It felt good to move my body and detox. I don't know if Grayson felt the same. He might as well have had a private class. For the entire ninety-minute class, the instructor devoted her attention solely to him.

Amelia and I couldn't stop laughing when the class ended. Grayson went into the men's locker room, and we went into the women's one. We didn't know why the instructor focused so much on Grayson, but it gave us a good laugh.

As we were packing our bags and exiting the locker room, the instructor stopped us. We were still wearing our sweaty leggings, sports bras, and t-shirts. She looked us up and down, baffled that we were about to walk outside in the cold without changing.

She told us that we couldn't leave before we rubbed ice on our skin. Amelia and I looked at each other and shrugged. "Okay, we'll do it."

I stood in the locker room in my underwear and sports bra, rubbing my sweaty body with ice chips. Amelia did the same. Since I was wetter than before, I decided, for once, that I would change into regular clothes since I had them in my backpack with me. I took off my sports bra and was about to put on a clean shirt when the instructor reappeared at my side.

I stood topless in front of her as she insisted I must take a shower before leaving; otherwise, I would most definitely get sick. *What do you do when you're standing half-naked in front of a determined Ukrainian woman telling you what to do?* We exited the locker room and met Grayson, who had been sitting in the lobby for fifteen minutes. The tables had turned; he was the one laughing this time.

A NEW KIND OF FAMILY

Despite the shortcomings of our hostel, excitement and happiness filled our room. It was Thanksgiving morning after all. With the company of friends and a second Couchsurfing experience under my travel belt, the feeling of culture shock had vanished as quickly as it came.

I sat on the top bunk, enjoying my second cappuccino after the yoga class and reflecting on how quickly I had settled back into the nuances of life in Ukraine. I felt good. I wasn't stressed about taking time off from teaching, feeling guilty about missing my family, or worrying about what I needed to do or where I needed to be next. *When was the last time I allowed myself to just relax and enjoy where I was?*

Morning turned into early afternoon. Our Thanksgiving party was in less than three hours, and we had a mandatory Fulbright meeting to attend beforehand. I was riding the high of that energy and laughing with my friends when I realized I was still in the clothes I had thrown on at the yoga studio. I jumped down from the top bunk, slipped on my shower shoes, and headed down the hall to the all-too-familiar hostel shower experience.

I chose one of three outfits I had been rotating on my week-long trip: a black turtleneck, a pleated skirt, tights, and combat boots. I put on a little extra mascara; it was a holiday after all.

I topped off my makeup with red lips as one friend shouted, "Everyone ready?"

Even though we had a work meeting on Thanksgiving, we maintained our high energy; complaining about it wouldn't do us any good. We checked in with our program director and made our way to the restaurant for an early dinner.

Our program organized the event. I think we each dreamed that some version of our usual Thanksgiving dinner in the United States would be present here: mashed potatoes, turkey, stuffing, sweet potatoes, pie. On the surface, it tried to be, but the overwhelming turnout of a small space filled with hundreds of strangers, a lack of authentic American food, and a reality that Thanksgiving this year required networking instead of easy conversation with family struck us all.

On a typical day, we would've been excited to meet so many people. We had all traveled halfway across the world to live in a foreign place, so meeting people wasn't off-putting. However, the combination of networking and the creeping guilt of not being with our families began to drain the high energy that we felt hours before.

As the event came to a close, we thanked the host and left the party, determined to bounce back from our deflation and press a redo button on our Thanksgiving dinner. We found a restaurant and replaced the finger food we ignored at the party with a meal that filled our bellies.

We called and texted our families. Slowly, our complaints and disappointments turned into joy and celebration. We laughed with ease and drank into the night, toasting to a new kind of Thanksgiving, and with it, a new kind of family.

A FORGOTTEN PROMISE

After a Thanksgiving celebration filled with highs and lows, we were pushed back into our jobs as if the holiday never happened. The following day, our program required us to participate in a visit to a private school to see its facilities and volunteer with the children who attended classes there.

The school was located in the Zhytomyr region, about three hours from Kyiv. We took a private van there, arriving in a small village. The stench of manure and farm animals contrasted the modern buildings that made up the campus. The public school was founded by a Ukrainian millionaire who wanted to create a progressive model of education that differed from the standard across the country and could be a framework for educational reform in Ukraine.

The facilities included advanced technology, a robust liberal arts curriculum, three meals for students throughout the day, and housing for teachers. It was similar to what I'd imagine would be the result of combining American charter and boarding schools into one institution.

We ate lunch together in the cafeteria, toured the campus, taught a class to children, and sat on a panel for a question and answer session. The school was progressive for Ukraine; there was no argument there.

It was interesting to see an example of a change in Ukraine, but something felt off. As we were pushed from classroom to classroom, I felt like a body that was simply filling the quota of being American, representing an ideal of whatever that meant in this context.

It was two hours after we were told we would be departing, yet we were still at the school. Finally, we finished our last meeting and were preparing to leave. A group of girls and I went to the bathroom before our long journey back to Kyiv. I went to the sink to wash my hands, taking off the ring I had been wearing since volunteering at the summer camp near Lviv in June, five months prior. A tan line left its mark around my left ring finger.

As I was washing my hands, I couldn't shake the feeling of being disingenuous. If you are volunteering your time and energy into something, I believe it has to come from a place of service and authenticity, not someone telling you that you are required to do it. I was trying to humble myself and remember that part of my job was doing what we did today.

We met back up with the group that was waiting for us near the exit. My right hand reached to twist the metal band that had taken up space and meaning on my left finger over the last few months. The ring was gone.

I ran, retracing my steps to the bathroom. I prayed the ring was where I left it and that someone didn't find it before I arrived.

I breathed a sigh of relief as I slid the ring back on. At one point in time, this token represented the promise of two people building a relationship in the simple moments – walking through the forest away from the rest of the world, watching the stars together and sharing stories of our lives, and aligning our words and actions with shared values. It represented a promise that didn't hold up to the reality of two people who fell for one another from different countries, cultures, and life paths.

The person I fell in love with that summer was no longer

in my life. Looking at the ring he gave me was a constant reminder of what didn't exist anymore.

We arrived back in Kyiv and returned to our hostel. I slipped the ring off and placed it in my locker. Love existed, but it existed in my heart and in the present moment of those around me.

HOSPITALITY

After experiencing two overwhelmingly positive Couchsurfing stays and a "Friendsgiving" dinner at a colleague's cozy apartment in Kyiv, I began to understand the importance of practicing hospitality.

While my apartment had come a long way since those first mice-ridden, furniture-free days, it still felt sparse. It was the apartment of a traveler who didn't spend enough time there.

I wanted my apartment to feel like my home away from home, and I wanted guests to feel that way too. I had been dreaming of hosting a dinner party for the Fulbrighters. I also dreamed of having students over to play card games, drink coffee, and practice English. I was hoping that maybe by improving my apartment space, I could slow down and spend more time in my host city.

I developed a mood board of photos: fashion, quotes, and color swatches. I found the local print center, printed 100 photos on stock paper, and created an accent wall. It represented me as soon as you walked into my flat. It was bold, creative, and spoke for itself.

I decorated my balcony, buying two orange corduroy stools to match the colorful Aztec rug and wooden table already there. In the spring and summer months, I planned for this to become my morning coffee oasis, a place where I could have a moment of silence or share a cup of coffee with a guest.

I bought seat cushions to cover my worn-out kitchen stools and a woven floor pouf to create more seating in my small living space. With my balcony and kitchen stools, plus my couch and new pouf, I could seat ten people.

It was ready. I was proud of my small but mighty space all over again.

A part of me knew two things: 1) Even though I created this space, I would still be drawn to traveling and have to make a conscious choice to stay in Zhytomyr, and 2) I didn't need to do any of this to practice hospitality.

Hospitality is more than a perfectly designed home with everything in order; it's more than having all the right things in all the right places.

Hospitality is a home-cooked meal, a thoughtful gift, a hand-written card – a feeling of being welcomed just as you are.

I had experienced each of those since living in Ukraine: visiting friends and staying in their village homes, eating home-cooked *varenyky* (pierogi), receiving a hand-written card from Irena's daughter upon my arrival, and being welcomed into my Zhytomyr community exactly how I was, whether I had a "nice" apartment or not.

I walked through my apartment, gliding my hand slowly across the collage pictures in my bedroom, gazing out the window of the balcony as passersby walked through the market, and pausing in the kitchen.

Let all that you do be done in love.

The quote from 1 Corinthians 16:14 was printed on my wall, a decal I had brought with me from the United States.

The answer to hospitality was right in front of me.

FIVE-STAR VIEW

When I first started apartment hunting in Zhytomyr, I created a list of the features that I hoped to find in a flat, the most important one being a central location. I wanted to be in the heart of the city, close enough to walk to work, to have easy access to a grocery store, and to see life happening around me. I wanted to feel the energy of the city.

I found just that. I loved my little apartment and my new decorations, faults and all. It was the first apartment I rented on my own. It was all mine, and there was no greater feeling.

Each morning before class, I made myself an espresso and heated soy milk to make a homemade latte. As I waited for the espresso to brew, I would lean on the windowsill and look outside. As the sun rose, I would slowly watch the market come alive. It was my favorite part of the day, and it went a little like this.

First, the permanent sellers would roll boxes of fruits and vegetables from their storage sheds behind my apartment and fill their tables with a mix of local and imported produce. The next scene that took place was what really drew me to my window every morning: the Ukrainian grandmas. Slowly, the grandmas would trickle in one at a time, sometimes two by two, some older than others. The older ones shocked me the most as their strength amazed me. I would often see them carrying two or three heavily packed totes, filled with goods they brought in hopes of selling that day.

The earliest arrivals would get the best spot next to the entrance, or so it seemed. I drank my latte and wondered if they had an unspoken agreement about who got to stand where. As the morning continued, more and more grandmas would flow in, filling up and breathing life into the market street.

By the time I walked outside to go to my first class, I would see up to fifty grandmas standing on the street. Each one would place a small square cloth on the cracked sidewalk to display their products: unshelled walnuts, fresh eggs, unpasteurized milk in reused Coke bottles, homemade farmer's cheese, butchered chickens wrapped in plastic bags, and beans in glass jars. These products were accompanied by local and seasonal fruit and vegetables grown in their gardens: berries and tomatoes in the warmer months and pumpkins and apples in the colder months.

The grandmas lined both edges of the sidewalk. I loved walking past them, trying to blend in with the crowds as the grandmas pointed to their produce and shouted what they were offering. I smiled at that sight every morning.

During the first week of December, I invited three of my students over for coffee at my flat. As I was brewing espresso for them, I stood at my usual position against the windowsill, gazing at the market. One of them noticed my position and joined.

"You have a five-star view of Zhytomyr," she said.

Laughter filled my kitchen; she was joking. To one person, living near the market might have been the worst place in the city to live. There were always crowds. There was garbage littered on the streets and stray dogs that wandered in packs. There was noise at all hours of the day and night.

I looked out that window again and smelled the fresh aroma of espresso filling my kitchen. It would always be a five-star view to me.

MISCOMMUNICATION

My faith suffered in Ukraine, or rather, I suffered because of my lack of faith. I went into my Fulbright experience having the strongest faith I've ever had, despite leaving my elderly father and other hardships. I was confident in all things through the lens of God.

I went to Mass every Sunday in Zhytomyr and in whatever city I was traveling to on the weekends. Even though my faith was next to nothing by December, I continued to attend Mass each week. I was disconnected, distrusting, and unfaithful, but I still showed up.

My church community at Saint John's was welcoming and devout. I arrived in Zhytomyr on a Saturday night in September and showed up to Mass the following morning. Each Sunday, the church was filled with only standing room in the back. Week after week, I joined those in the back, representative of my distanced and declining relationship with God.

One Sunday in October, I discovered the church had a little gift shop filled with prayer cards, religious icons, and rosaries. The following weekend, I would be flying to Rome to meet my brother, a seminarian, and four other seminarians to witness the canonization of Saint John

Henry Newman. I wanted to buy each seminarian a prayer card.

I walked into the small shop and sifted through the prayer cards. All of the cards were written in Polish. I was searching for a card written in Ukrainian.

Using Google Translate, I asked the woman behind the register if she had any prayer cards in Ukrainian.

I don't know how my question translated, but she led me to a back room where I met my friend, Alex, who spoke English, and a priest. The woman disappeared back to the gift shop.

Confused, I explained to Alex that I was trying to buy a few prayer cards. She told the priest, and he asked me for the name of the person I wanted to request a Mass to be said for.

I told him my brother's name, which he transliterated into Ukrainian.

I walked back to the gift shop, bought five prayer cards in Polish, and made my way back to my apartment. I opened my agenda and wrote the date and time of the Mass that would be said for my brother.

December 9 – I sat in a pew in the back of the church as usual. It was the last place I wanted to be on a busy Monday night. Two months after trying to buy prayer cards, I begrudgingly sat in a cold church thanks to a miscommunication.

As I sat in the church, following the structure of the Mass but not understanding the words, I thought about that miscommunication. It had led me to the last place I wanted to be, but the place I needed to be at most. This book doesn't speak about my faith or Christianity.

It doesn't speak about it because I was a poor disciple and a poor example of the faith in many ways. My time in Ukraine challenged my faith many times; sometimes my faith won, and other times I succumbed to the false promises of this Earth.

My nose was running and my hands were cold. God could work through me even through the unfaithful moments, and the outcome of His mercy and grace would be an outcome far greater than anything of this world.

STILLNESS OF A DECEMBER MEMORY

When I lay awake at night, I find my thoughts drifting to Ukraine. It begins with memories of my host city, my colleagues, and travels with friends. These memories are etched into the corners of my mind; it is as if I could open my eyes and return to the exact moment and place they happened.

I often wonder if we're meant to meet certain people in our lives. If we're meant to make decisions the way we did. I believe in a God who has a plan for me. Maybe God was the one who brought you into my life, but good or bad, I made the decision to keep you in it.

There's a picture of us laughing together in the summer. I don't know what we were talking about, but our smiles tell me it was something funny, probably something you said. You had a way of making me forget my serious nature. I was living a life analyzing the best options, setting and achieving high goals, and committing to a never-ending reach of perfectionism. But to you, life was an adventure. You were riding the waves of life around you with ease, with happiness, and with a spirit I admired.

I wanted to be part of that ease, and with you around, the wave encompassed me. I felt lighter, the pressure stacked on my shoulders slowly melted away. I felt creative and connected. I always wondered how you did it. *Did you choose to let go of the gravities around you? Did you seek happiness and forget the rest? Were you hurting inside and hiding it from the outside world?*

The more time I spent with you, the more I got to know you. We explored new places and laughed the kind of deep belly laughs that make you feel alive again. We drank coffee and planned our next adventure. We spent hours together discussing our walks of life: our faith, beliefs, families, and future dreams.

Over the years, I've learned that traveling heightens emotions: the highs become higher, the lows become lower, the passion becomes deeper, and the discontent becomes more expressed. Maybe that's why this memory repeats itself in the stillness of late nights – a memory of two souls who were connected for moments in time and meant to fade back into their separate lives. Maybe it repeats itself because it's a memory that transcended each time we met again.

I think about the twenty-four hours of that December day so vividly. I watched you turn your back as you walked into the metro station, onto your next destination as always. I wanted to run after you and say the words I couldn't bring myself to say before. *How is it that I knew you, but felt like there was always more?* I knew the parts of you that you showed me in the memories we shared, and I knew the parts of you that I wanted to believe in. I wanted to believe that the smiles of that summer photograph held more than a happenstance of two people crossing paths. Maybe God was the one who brought you into my life, but good or bad, I made the decision to let go.

When I lay awake at night, I find my thoughts drifting to Ukraine. No matter how vibrant those memories are, I always come back to one memory: *you*.

BACK, BACK AGAIN

There were many sleepless nights in my apartment in Zhytomyr. While in Ukraine, I slept sporadically, waking up four or five times per night and often only sleeping for a total of five or six hours. I credit my poor sleep schedule to a mix of the anxiety of living alone in a foreign country, worry about being far away from my ninety-four-year-old father, and excitement for too many travel and lesson plans. Living above a store with an alarm that went off daily at seven o'clock in the morning didn't help either.

Some nights were good; I would dream, returning to the list of goals I wrote for the dean months prior. I would cycle through my ideas of conferences, speaking topics for my classes and clubs, articles for my blog, and travel plans with friends. I would dream about visiting all corners of Ukraine: the war-torn East, the majestic mountain ranges, the Black Sea, and my students' villages.

Other nights I felt I was drowning; I would fear my father passing away suddenly while I was selfishly traveling the world, I would repeat my failure to learn Ukrainian and Russian, and I would convince myself I wasn't doing enough for my students or community.

This night was neither good nor bad. It was mid-December and my room was frigid, the regulated central heating temperature for the building often very low. I laid awake in bed, under layers of blankets, unable to sleep.

By one o'clock in the morning, I gave up on any notion

of resting. If I was going to be awake anyway, I would do work to get ahead for the week. I slid out of the comfort of my warm bed and walked into my dark kitchen, something I rarely did because of the cockroaches.

I wanted a piece of chocolate to munch on, a bad habit I formed in Ukraine. I stored all of my food in the refrigerator, even non-perishables, because of the cockroaches. I turned on the kitchen lights, opened the fridge, and broke off a piece of dark chocolate.

As I closed the refrigerator door, I was met face-to-face with a cockroach two inches above the fridge door handle. My appetite was gone. I threw the chocolate away in the trash can and ran to the hallway to grab a shoe. By the time I returned to the kitchen, the cockroach had positioned itself inside the door handle, along the crack of the refrigerator opening.

I knew the shoe couldn't fit inside the handle, but there was no way I was killing a cockroach with a paper towel and my bare hands. I smacked the door with the shoe as hard as I could.

The cockroach disappeared. I looked on the floor, behind the refrigerator, on the bottom of my shoe, and even inside the refrigerator. I checked a second time before giving up.

I don't know where the cockroach went. I don't know if it was alive or dead that night. At that moment, I knew one and only one thing: it was time for me to find a new apartment and move on. I was done. I was done with the sleepless nights, the cockroaches and the mice, the sketchy market area at night, and the daily alarm from the store below me. No amount of Ukrainian hospitality, discount on rent, or cockroach traps could change my mind.

I drifted to sleep, engulfed in thoughts of cockroaches and dreaming of a new beginning.

CHILDHOOD NOSTALGIA

During our Thanksgiving dinner, I met a new friend named Roma, a Ukrainian-American who was studying ballet and dance in Kyiv. He was kind-hearted and friendly, the kind of guy you knew was a gentleman from the start.

We talked about ballet that night. He showed me photos from previous shows he danced in and I told him of my childhood memories of taking ballet lessons until age fourteen. It was nostalgic to think about those recitals and graceful afternoons spent in the studio. We agreed that night that we would attend a ballet in Kyiv in the upcoming weeks.

It was a cold December morning. My bags were packed for my flight home on December 19. I would spend the next two nights in Kyiv, one night attending the ballet at the Opera House, and one night staying at a hotel close to the airport.

I woke up excited for the day ahead. I purchased a gown and scheduled a hair and makeup appointment to prepare for the ballet. It felt good to have an excuse to get dressed up.

Aside from my nails, I found everything else I needed in Zhytomyr by asking my students and colleagues or by searching on Instagram. I searched #ZhytomyrMakeup and scrolled through talented artists to find a makeup artist, messaging a few to see if they had any availability. It was a win-win for me because I could see their work in advance and I could message them directly to avoid any miscommunication in person.

I found a trendy salon and made an appointment through Instagram. I nervously entered the salon, knowing I would stand out as an American as soon as I spoke. I spent the next two hours being pampered. The beauty industry in Ukraine is an animal in itself; the quality is unmatchable, the detail is exquisite, and the price is low (compared to American prices).

I got a fresh haircut, curls, and a full face of makeup including lashes for forty dollars. I was shocked at how low the price was for what I received, but I'm not here to talk about money. What was special about that day was meeting the stylists. It was just like meeting Irina when I got my nails done for the first time. The young women at the salon were welcoming, they made me feel comfortable, and they became familiar faces. We followed each other on Instagram and we drank coffee (some form of coffee is always involved in Ukrainian hospitality). I would return every few weeks to get my eyebrows done there.

Some people may say that these are luxuries not worth spending money on while traveling or living abroad, or that time should be spent doing something more important. One could make that argument; however, I would argue that it was more than hair and nails. I loved going to Irina's apartment and going to that salon to see familiar faces, to drink coffee together, and to learn more about my host city. Getting beauty treatments done was a pathway for me to meet locals and feel like part of the community.

I arrived at the Opera House and met Roma. We took our seats on the balcony and enjoyed a nostalgic night at the ballet together.

READY OR NOT, HERE I GO

When I left the United States in August, I informed my family with a heavy heart that I wouldn't be coming home for the holidays. During my previous trips abroad, I had always journeyed home for Christmas and New Year's. While I was grateful to see my family during that time, I was left with a whirlwind of emotions and dreaded the part where we had to say goodbye again. We did it once, *why were we putting ourselves through the same painstaking goodbye again?* My decision was selfish, but I wanted to commit myself to Ukraine. I wanted to experience Ukrainian Christmas traditions, I wanted extra time to travel, and I didn't want to relive that August day when I left my family.

It was the morning of December 18. I received a confirmation email from United Airlines. My flight to New York City was on schedule for the following day. I left my suitcase at the hostel, asking the staff to hold it for the day while I spent time in the city. I knew my flight was leaving early, so I decided a few weeks prior that I wanted to spend the night near the airport. I messaged a host on Couchsurf and she kindly accepted my request.

I had ten hours to kill before I could arrive at my host's accommodation. I spent the morning at a cafe near the Opera House, caught up on my journaling from the last few weeks, and went to a few local stores to buy Christmas gifts for family and friends. I had a fancier lunch than usual and spent the afternoon in another cafe.

While I was at the second cafe, I tried to log into my Couchsurfing account on my phone. I received an error message. I tried again and the same thing happened. I needed to access my inbox so I could ask the host for her address and inform her what time I would be arriving. I went back to the hostel and tried to log in again on my laptop. The same thing happened.

I didn't want to break the unspoken rule of Couchsurfing and ditch my host without an explanation, but I needed a place to sleep. I Googled hotels on my laptop. I could spend the extra money, book a hotel near the airport, and hope my Couchsurfing host would accept my apologies when I gained access to my account again. Much to my surprise, I received another error message on my browser.

My anxiety heightened. I spent all day walking around the city because I didn't have any other place to go. I arranged a place to stay that night and trusted this stranger. I abandoned my own decision not to go home for the sake of my family, for my ninety-four-year-old father, who was worth more than a few extra travel days in Ukraine.

I went outside for some fresh air. My chest felt tight, but I kept walking. With each step, it became increasingly harder to breathe. I walked a few more blocks before I realized I had begun to hold my chest and wheeze. I sat on the concrete sidewalk. I looked around at all the strangers passing me as a wave of nausea overcame me. The strangers blurred into obscurity as my vision faded to blackness.

I had a panic attack alone on a sidewalk during rush hour in Kyiv. It wasn't the first time I had experienced a travel-related panic attack. I knew it as it was happening, but I couldn't stop it. It didn't happen because I didn't have a Couchsurfing host or hotel to stay at. I could've asked a friend or a family member to try to log into my Couchsurfing account or book another accommodation for me. There were hundreds of hostels and hotels I could've stayed at in Kyiv.

I had a panic attack because I was going home.

I wrote online that day: "I was nineteen when I moved abroad for the first time, and I've been traveling for much of my life since then. After each journey, it never gets easier to return home to the place you've decided to leave. You yearn for the familiarity of your friends, your family, the streets and the cafes you know like the back of your hand. Yet you know in many ways that you've outgrown it, that you've become a newer version of yourself who is now trying to fit inside a place that no longer understands you in the same light. Just like when you left, you push onward and trust in what awaits you on the other side."

Slowly, I regained my breath, forcing my body to push onward and trust in what awaited me on the other side.

AN UNOPENED LETTER

When I was packing my bags for my trip home in December, my Ukrainian tutor, Iryna, asked me to do her a favor. She wouldn't accept any form of payment from me for our previous lessons, so the least I could do for her was to say yes. She handed me a package and told me a story.

Iryna and her husband had crossed paths with an American man who had traveled to Zhytomyr years ago. His name was Ted and his wife was from Ukraine. He visited Ukraine many times and had a great love for the country, but hadn't been back in the years since his wife had passed away. He was now in his seventies or eighties and living in his hometown in Alabama. He and Iryna had fallen out of contact; she only had his last known address and email.

"Can you send this package to Ted?" she asked. It would be cheaper and easier for me to ship it from the United States.

Along with a letter, she included his favorite Ukrainian chocolate and Belarusian condensed milk. Iryna's husband was Belarusian and had introduced him to it.

I was happy to do a favor for someone who had given up so much of their free time to teach me.

I sent the gift as soon as I arrived in New Jersey on December 19. I wondered if this elderly man would be wary of opening a package from a stranger in New Jersey (the package showed my return address). *Would I open something from a stranger?*

When I returned to Ukraine, Iryna told me that Ted had emailed her saying that he received the care package. It was such a simple thing, but I felt so much joy witnessing two people rekindle a friendship even after many years had passed.

I arrived home a few months later and spent the next few months writing this book while readjusting to life in the United States. It was a typical day when my mom came into my office and handed me a letter.

She apologized, "I'm sorry, this got mixed in with my mail."

While I was gone, my family had been collecting my mail and leaving it in my room. I sorted through the dusty pile that lay dormant on my nightstand. This letter hadn't made it to the pile.

It was dated December 31, 2019, and was addressed by a man named Ted from Alabama. It's not often that a Jersey girl interacts with someone from Alabama. I was wondering who I knew there and it hit me; Iryna's friend! I assumed it was a letter for her. I would open it and send her a text with a picture of what he wrote.

I opened the letter. Its contents read:

> *Kat,*
>
> *I appreciate you helping with the chocolate. I really loved it. I don't think it's proper for you to pay postage so enclosed is money to repay you.*
>
> > *Thanks,*
> > *Ted*

Enclosed with the letter was a crisp twenty dollar bill. What Ted didn't know was that when he sent me that letter and money, I was writing this book. I sent him a copy of the book you're reading now. Iryna wouldn't let me pay for my Ukrainian lessons and Ted wouldn't let me pay for the shipping that was way less than the twenty dollars he included. Their kindness taught me, one person at a time, that goodness goes farther than any amount of money.

WHAT COMES AROUND GOES AROUND

I had a panic attack leaving Ukraine in December and I had a panic attack returning a week later. It was the day after my birthday, December 27. I had a red-eye flight to Vienna and then a second flight to Kyiv, where my two friends from the United States would be meeting me.

I paid extra for an aisle seat, a habit I had formed after my first panic attack on a flight to China in 2016. I had a middle seat on that flight and I told myself I would always choose the aisle seat in case it happened again. I'd be able to move freely, have easy access to the bathroom, and get help quickly if I couldn't breathe or fainted.

There was a passenger in the middle seat next to me and a middle-aged woman in the window seat. I was mentally and emotionally drained from the roller coaster of going home. When I was in New Jersey, I was constantly racing against the clock, and losing every minute. *How do you spend enough time with your ninety-four-year-old father when you know you'll be leaving in six days?* Saying goodbye to him sent me on another drop on the roller coaster.

Guilt and anxiety overwhelmed me as I boarded the plane. I took a nausea pill when I got to my seat and placed a plastic bag in the sleeve in front of me in case the pill didn't do its job. I rolled lavender oil on my temples to try to ease my anxiety.

I was seconds away from putting my head on the tray table and drowning my guilt out with music when the woman two seats away from me started up a conversation. I didn't want to talk to a stranger, not now. I didn't want to explain why I was on a plane to Vienna and I didn't want to be reminded that I left my father behind once again.

I set my headphones down and forced a response. She was from the United States and had been teaching as a professor in Vienna for many years. I told her that I was on my way back to Ukraine to continue in my own teaching position. We continued our conversation and I told her my goal of wanting to become a travel writer someday. Our lives spanned years apart, but we had similar interests in international teaching and travel. I gave her my email in case we crossed paths again. As our plane took off, our conversation lulled and I soon drifted to sleep.

I awoke to a violent wave of nausea. I looked at the clock on the screen in front of me; we were only halfway through our ten-hour journey. I felt beads of sweat pool at the back of my neck and on the temples of my forehead. My hands started to cramp, my breath shortened, and my vision blurred.

Not again, I thought to myself through the spells of faintness. I was having a panic attack for the second time in a week. I grabbed the plastic bag in front of me and stuck my head inside it for the next hour as I tried to gain control of my nausea and release the tightness in my chest.

The woman in the window seat noticed something was wrong and asked me if I was okay. I don't remember if she or I asked the flight attendant for ginger ale, but it appeared before me and I was thankful to have something to calm my stomach. I was even more thankful to have someone watching out for me.

When we finally landed, I thanked the woman again for her kindness and wished her well. She suggested I go to a doctor when I arrived in Kyiv, but I knew my lingering symptoms would pass by then.

A few weeks later, I received an email in my inbox. It was from Lisa, the woman on the plane. Her kindness extended from Vienna to Kyiv. She asked about my health and encouraged me to continue writing.

> *I visited your website - read some of your posts - you are a great writer! And what a smile you have. I bet you could turn your experience in Ukraine into some great short stories or a book. Have you thought of that? For people in the U.S., Ukraine is so far away and foreign...*

I guess you could say she had a good idea, huh?

INTERNATIONAL TRIO

I arrived in Kyiv on December 28. Eighteen hours had passed from the time I left my New Jersey home. I passed through customs, always relieved when there wasn't a problem with my Ukrainian residence permit. I walked to the baggage claim area, watching one bag after another tumble down the ramp by its heaviness. After my panic attack on the flight, I felt the same weight of those bags; I had tumbled and been brought down by my own heaviness.

Memories of my first impressions of Kyiv played as I wheeled my suitcase to the familiar terminal. When I arrived in the city in September, I was alone and didn't know if I had made the right decision to come to Ukraine. This time, although I still felt guilty, I knew I was returning to a community of friendships and familiarity. Not only did I have the gift of knowing I wasn't alone, I also had the joy of two friends arriving in Kyiv from the United States right behind me.

I sat in the terminal, patiently and eagerly checking the arrival board for my friends' flights. When the board signaled their respective arrivals, I joined the crowd of other eager friends and family holding flowers and balloons. I unfolded a piece of paper and held it with two hands:

"Welcome to Ukraine!" was written and accompanied by an American flag and a Ukrainian flag.

I don't think my friends even saw the paper. I dropped it as I ran to them and hugged them as tight as I could. Their friendship was a light in my life in America and continued to be at a moment when I needed it most in Ukraine. We hugged again and again, and slowly my guilt began to melt away.

We stood by the crowds, gathering our bags and trying to contain our excitement. Seeing them in person brought me more joy than I imagined. We were really in Ukraine together again.

This was the third time we were in Ukraine together. I met Aubrey and Callie in the summer of 2018. Aubrey was from Virginia, Callie was from Nevada, and I was from New Jersey, yet we all ended up as volunteer English teachers at the same summer camp in a small village outside Lviv. The camp left a lasting impression on us and we returned in 2019. Both summers were filled with singing and dancing around bonfires, teaching English to Ukrainian students who were the same age as us, praying in the chapel, staying up late telling stories, hammocking in the forest, and building our friendship.

On July 14, 2019, the three of us met in our outdated camp room. We were sitting on my bed with a stack of papers spread across the comforter. I grabbed a pen from the nightstand and looked at both of them, asking, "Do you think I'm crazy if I do this?"

I signed my name on the paper – the contract for my Fulbright. I was going to teach English in Ukraine for nine months.

Callie traveled fifty hours and Aubrey traveled twenty to visit me in Kyiv. They traveled to support me just like they had supported when I signed those papers. Our first meeting was by chance, our second was by individual choice, and our third was a choice we made together. These weren't just any kind of friends, they were friends I could count on anywhere in the world, especially in Ukraine.

OVERFLOW

We were exhausted, each having been awake and traveling for over a day. Callie, Aubrey, and I had fallen asleep on our bus from Kyiv to Zhytomyr. It was late evening on December 28 when we finally arrived at my apartment.

I hadn't been in my apartment since December 18, before I flew home to the United States. My keys felt strange in my hand. I couldn't remember how many times to turn the top lock and how many times to turn the bottom lock. *How could I have forgotten that quickly?*

It was a strange feeling, yet joyful beyond what words could express, to have my two best friends from the United States standing in my little Zhytomyr apartment.

"I can't believe you are both really here!" I repeated over and over again.

Fighting sleep, we discussed our upcoming travel plans. We would spend three days in Lviv, seeing our friends from the summer camp where we all taught English and celebrating New Year's there. After, we would spend two days in Zhytomyr and one night in Kyiv.

I booked our bus tickets to and from each destination. To maximize our time, I booked a ten-dollar overnight bus from Zhytomyr to Lviv. Our bus was leaving at one o'clock in the morning that night. We would arrive in Lviv at seven o'clock on December 29.

Four hours of sleepiness stood between us and our bus ride. We all needed to shower, feeling grimy from our long day of travels. I showed Callie and Aubrey how to use my shower. Yes, I did, in fact, need to explain how to use my shower.

After living in my apartment for four months, I could have made a lengthy list of all the problems: mice, faulty electricity, cockroaches, water outages, and a faulty bathtub.

Yet, despite the problems, I was still grateful for my little space and had gotten used to the faults, including the tub. It was an old claw-foot style tub with a metal barrier on the outside to hide the "feet" and whatever was underneath the tub. The shower curtain needed to be placed perfectly so as not to flood the bathroom. The shower head was handheld, making shampooing and washing difficult without a place to hang it.

Callie and Aubrey finished showering. As I walked into the bathroom, I wondered if there would be any hot water left or if any water would even come out of the showerhead. (Without notice, the water supply to my apartment would often shut off for hours.)

Anticipating the worst, I was shocked to have met a different sight. The floors were flooded. The bathmat was soaked. Water was under the tub, around the toilet, and over the tiles.

I walked back into my room where Callie and Aubrey were sitting. I couldn't be mad. We looked at each other in silence before bursting into laughter.

It didn't matter if I had to clean up my bathroom and that I still lived in an unpredictable apartment. My two best friends were in my new home. They spent money and time to see me. That's what mattered. I smiled to myself as the cold water dripped down my back and the metal tub barrier toppled onto the tile.

LET IT SNOW

After being awake for over thirty hours, and even longer for Callie and Aubrey, it was time to go to the bus station. It was midnight, and our bus was set to leave at one o'clock in the morning. We re-packed our belongings for our New Year's trip to Lviv, leaving some items behind for our return to Zhytomyr.

I locked my apartment, the keys feeling more familiar than they did hours before. Using our flashlights for guidance, we descended the dark, concrete stairwell of my Soviet-style apartment. I opened the metal door to the outside, hoping no one would be up and awake at this hour. A pit was growing in my stomach at the thought of traveling during the night, a travel rule I rarely broke.

We were met with snow, and lots of it. There were flurries every which way and soon, on every surface of our bodies. We rushed to the taxi waiting on the street in front of my apartment. He drove us through the snowy roads to the bus station.

I warned Callie and Aubrey that it usually took me a few minutes, maybe longer, to find the correct bus. I told them not to worry if it took me some time; we'd find it.

Normally filled with coach buses, marshrutkas, and travelers, the bus station was deserted and eerie. It was a sight I had never seen before.

We waited in the warmth of the waiting room, where I checked the bus timetables. Our bus wasn't listed, a usual occurrence. We waited for half an hour until we began to see other passengers.

A bus had pulled up to the deserted lot. Aubrey and Callie

waited as I ran to read the sign in the windshield, careful not to slip on the icy snow that had coated the road. It wasn't our bus.

We waited as the clock neared our departure time. I was too exhausted to worry. I booked our bus; it should arrive, and if not, we could go back to my apartment.

At exactly one o'clock in the morning, another bus pulled into the lot. This time, we all went outside to read the name. I breathed a sigh of relief knowing we would be out of the cold, sleep was near, and our journey to Lviv was on track.

I couldn't stop shivering. There was no heat on the bus. Sleep was intermittent as the bus drove over ill-paved, slippery, and snowy roads.

We stopped in Rivne at four o'clock in the morning, a city halfway between Zhytomyr and Lviv. I was familiar with the city, having visited a few weeks prior and having stopped here on my last bus ride to Lviv. I knew we would be waiting for half an hour for new passengers.

The bus door remained open for thirty minutes. The cold was biting. I looked around me, trying to do anything to distract myself from the cold. Everyone else was sleeping. The driver was outside smoking a cigarette as the snow continued to fall. It seemed like a typical night for everyone.

An overnight bus is an experience that sounds wise at first; it's cheaper and saves time by traveling during a time when you would normally be sleeping anyway. Yet, when you're on an overnight bus, there is nothing wise about it; it's uncomfortable, it's exhausting, and it's mentally challenging to stay positive. Maybe that's where the real wisdom is discovered: experiencing budget traveling and pushing yourself a little further each and every time.

BOOM DYNAMITE

The snow was a few inches deep, and the sunrise hadn't broken through the darkness when we arrived at the main bus station in Lviv. My body was shivering, exacerbated by my tiredness. I knew which bus would bring us to the city center where we could find a cafe to warm up.

It was a little after seven o'clock in the morning when we arrived downtown. I had never been in the city center that early before, and neither had Callie or Aubrey. Most coffee shops weren't open yet. Callie and Aubrey wanted to grab breakfast and I happily agreed if coffee was promised.

We sat down at a table in an empty restaurant. When the waitress arrived, I ordered my usual morning coffee: a cappuccino.

"We don't have cappuccinos," the waitress responded.

I was groggy, still cold, and now disgruntled. A Ukrainian restaurant without coffee – that's a first.

I left Aubrey and Callie at the restaurant. I didn't want to bear the snowy winter day again just as I had begun to warm up, but coffee was calling my name.

I found a little shop across from the Opera House and weaved my way back through the side streets to meet Aubrey and Callie where I had left them.

We were exhausted, and it was only eight o'clock in the morning. We couldn't check into our Airbnb until two o'clock in the afternoon.

To keep ourselves awake, we took a bus to the university associated with the camp where we taught English the previous two summers. It was a strange sight to be there together in the winter. Long gone were the lush wildflowers, summer nights, and bonfires.

We walked around the campus, changed our clothes in one of the bathrooms, and went to Mass. If it was possible to fall asleep standing up, we did.

After Mass, we went to our favorite restaurant by the university. During the summer of 2019, my luggage was lost on my flight from Poland to Ukraine. I was supposed to arrive at the same time as Callie, Aubrey, and my brother, Allen. Due to my two-hour delay, they had long since arrived and had gone out to eat. I left the airport without my luggage and took a taxi to the restaurant. I remember the joy of walking through those restaurant doors, seeing my brother again, and seeing Aubrey and Callie in the place where our friendship started. "Love and Lviv Family Restaurant," a fitting name.

Our Airbnb host messaged me saying we could check into our apartment at last. Too tired to take public transportation, we ordered an Uber to the city center. The ride was only fifteen minutes, but we drifted into sleep.

My body jolted out of sleep towards the dashboard as Callie's and Aubrey's did the same. The sound was as loud as dynamite, two pieces of metal hitting one another at high speed. We didn't know what happened until we turned around.

Our tiny Uber was rear-ended by a full-size bus.

The driver exited the car once he determined the scene to be safe. Knowing how many times I had been yelled at by Ukrainian drivers in the past four months, I anticipated a loud argument to ensue. As the driver stood up, he whispered, not in Ukrainian, but in English, "Fuck."

The quietest fuck I ever heard. I couldn't hold in my

laughter, and neither could the driver as he looked at us. He shrugged and walked towards the bus driver, obviously never having experienced a situation quite like this. We took that as our cue to leave, reaching for our luggage over the backseat since the trunk was smashed against the bus. We waved goodbye, making our way to our Airbnb by foot and giving the driver a five-star review on Uber.

CELEBRATION

Each year, the holidays brought a pang of depression and nostalgia for me. Ever since I was a teenager, I felt this numbing sadness during Christmas, my birthday (the day after Christmas), and New Year's, a sadness that makes me want to slip away until the holidays are over. Maybe it's because we celebrate three different occasions in one week and there's not much else to celebrate during the rest of the year. Maybe it's because I have a heightened awareness of the goals I set out to accomplish but didn't achieve. Maybe I just envisioned the holidays to look differently.

New Year's Eve was here, a holiday that usually brought a cloud of depression over me. I never celebrated New Year's Eve any place but my home, a realization I had as we began planning our celebration in Lviv.

I wanted this year to be different. I wanted to smile as the clock hit midnight. I wanted to surround myself with happiness and joyful friends. I wanted to be out and about and feel like I was living. I wanted to break through the cocoon of depression that wrapped around me every holiday season.

I was in the right place to do just that.

Aubrey, Callie, and I spent the day meeting our Ukrainian friends for coffee and wandering through the old city of Lviv. We dressed up and had a fancy rooftop dinner, thanks to Aubrey's generous father. We met my Fulbright friend, Sydney, and a few more friends from the summer camp. My Fulbright world and Ukrainian summer camp world collided.

There was so much joy, so much laughter, so much alcohol, and so many reasons to be thankful.

After dinner, Sydney, Callie, Aubrey, and I faced the crowds. We wove our way through groups of friends and families, making our way to the square near the Opera House where the New Year's countdown was happening.

People in front of us. People behind us. People on our left and people on our right.

In every direction I looked, people were smiling. The joy of being exactly where I was in that moment felt serendipitous, a moment that had the power to break the wrap of depression around me.

...3, 2, 1.

Fireworks exploded, champagne bottles popped, and noise erupted from every corner of the square.

We hugged each other with gratitude for a new year and for the gift of being together. The neighboring couple popped a bottle of champagne, handed us glasses, and toasted to the New Year, giving us the rest of their bottle as a gift.

We cheered, we met up with friends, we drank homemade Ukrainian wine, and we let 2020 fill our hearts with hope, happiness, and gratitude; it was a year we promised would be unlike any other.

PRIVATE BUS

After a whirlwind of a trip to Lviv, I was excited to return to Zhytomyr to show Callie and Aubrey my home city. I booked us another bus, a six-hour trip eastward to Zhytomyr.

Even after living in Ukraine for four months, my biggest challenge while traveling was still finding the correct bus to my destination. There are private coach buses, international buses, local marshrutkas, intercity marshrutkas, and buses that even pick up passengers outside the bus station parameters.

I stressed, I searched, and I asked. I found a bus labeled Zhytomyr, assuming it was ours. No, it couldn't be that easy. I stressed, I searched, and I asked again and again before finally finding the correct bus. Bingo.

We boarded the fifteen-passenger minivan, a far cry from the coach bus we took overnight to Lviv. We took our seats in the front as I prayed my motion sickness would be mitigated.

The clock hit ten o'clock, our departure time. The three of us looked at one another, wondering why there were no other passengers on the bus. I had taken many buses in Ukraine, and this was a sight I had never seen.

The driver started the van and nodded at us, and off we went. It was odd to be the only passengers on the bus, but what was even more unusual was the sight of three Americans and a Ukrainian driver on the road to an unlikely tourist destination: Zhytomyr.

We giggled to ourselves about memories in Ukraine from the previous summers and memories from our trip so far.

We giggled that we had a private bus to Zhytomyr. We giggled that my two best friends were visiting a city they never thought they would have on their bucket lists.

The bus stayed empty for at least four hours. At each stop, we wondered if newcomers would join. Nobody boarded the bus.

We fell asleep on the winding, bumpy roads. My body jolted in fear again. This time, a pillow from the overhead compartment had landed on my lap. I chuckled to myself, knowing very well that there was never a day in Ukraine without surprises as I drifted back to sleep.

I woke up an hour later to a full bus. I looked at Callie and Aubrey in confusion.

"What happened to our private bus?" I asked jokingly.

We couldn't stop laughing. One moment we were eating Nutella and reminiscing about our trips in Ukraine, another moment a pillow scared me, and another moment everyone decided it was time to go to Zhytomyr.

I shrugged. Callie shrugged. Aubrey shrugged.

We knew one thing was certain from our travels in Ukraine in 2018, 2019, and now 2020: don't ask questions in Ukraine, just laugh, smile, and let the surprises roll off your shoulders.

DON'T TALK, WHISPER

Whenever I was with my Fulbright friend, he would point out that I whispered a lot in public, especially when we were on public transport or in cafes.

He asked, "Why do you always whisper, Kat? Most people probably can't understand what you're saying anyway."

I didn't whisper every conversation. I simply whispered words I didn't want people to hear: my reactions to the culture, my shock at surprises, my frustrations, and my observations. These were not necessarily negative comments, just differences I noticed.

My reasoning for whispering was twofold. Foremost, I didn't want to offend anyone with my comments. I have heard many travelers speaking English in foreign places where they think no one understands what they are saying, and the result is that local people can and do understand. If we look at this situation, the locals view the tourists as ignorant or insensitive and the tourists view the locals as a one-size-fits-all: no one speaks English here. Neither is a positive outcome, in my opinion. Secondly, I didn't want to mold into the stereotype that all Americans are loud. Maybe it's petty, but I didn't need an entire bus to know I was an American simply by the volume of my voice.

And so, my solution was to whisper.

It was New Year's Day, January 1, 2020. Aubrey, Callie, and I were in Zhytomyr. We were meeting Irena and her family for a celebratory dinner.

I anticipated meeting Irena, Valery, and Vlada as usual, but when we arrived outside the restaurant, there was a special guest.

Irena had told me stories about her son. He was my age, twenty-four years old. One of the most difficult periods of their life as a family was when he served in the Ukrainian army on the frontline during the height of the war. After his service, he had moved to Poland to continue his studies. He didn't come home very often; he was building a new life there.

Here he was, standing in front of us. I introduced myself and my two American friends, failing to hide my shock that he had returned to Ukraine. The last time he had come home was two years ago; this wasn't an ordinary day.

We sat down at a table that fit the seven of us. Irena's family was on one side of the table, and my friends and I were on the opposite. Our conversation was lively, but Irena's son was quiet. He had introduced himself in English, but he didn't say one word for the first twenty minutes of our dinner. He simply smiled when we smiled and laughed when we laughed.

As dinner continued, so did his silence. I wasn't sure if he understood our conversation or felt comfortable speaking English. As Irena's family was talking to each other in Ukrainian, I whispered to my friends, "He's cute!"

He was looking right at me.

I continued the conversation with the table, still not knowing if he spoke English. We finished our meal and walked outside through the local Christmas market. His quietness disappeared. He spoke English fluently, understanding every word I was saying. I could feel the heat rising in my cheeks. He knew exactly what I said at the dinner table.

Maybe whispering doesn't work so well after all.

HOLLOW

After two short days in Zhytomyr, it was time for our last destination: Kyiv. Our trip had come full circle to the place we started in six days prior. We booked a last-minute Airbnb in Kyiv for January 2, my mind flashing back to all the Airbnbs and hostels I had stayed in throughout the city since my arrival in September.

Kyiv was a second host city for me. Only two hours away from Zhytomyr, I spent many of my weekends there, exploring downtown and using the city as a launching point to travel to cities around Ukraine and neighboring countries. I knew the city well: the coffee shops that offered vegan milk options, American breakfast spots, the most authentic Chinese food I could find, and shops for souvenirs and clothes.

On each street, a memory of a different person flashed through my mind. A sight I saw with that person, a day I spent with that person, a coffee I drank with that person. I thought of my life in America and my life now. I was filled with gratitude for all that Ukraine had offered to me thus far.

We built onto those memories for one last night together. I took Aubrey and Callie to the Friendship Arch and Maidan. We walked Khreshchatyk Street, which was lined with shops and beautiful buildings. We ate Chinese food at my favorite little hole-in-the-wall restaurant and drank sea buckthorn tea, a staple winter drink in Ukraine.

It didn't feel like my two best friends were leaving in less than twelve hours. As we explored Kyiv, I was wrapped in happiness with my two best friends by my side: one on my left and one on my right. Yet, in that happiness, I knew the impending loneliness would creep into my mind soon enough.

In twelve hours, I would be alone in Ukraine again: living alone, facing surprises alone, and trying to make sense of my little life here alone.

I was sad, but I tried not to let my sadness impede our last few hours together. We laughed as hard as we laughed on the first day we were together, on New Year's Eve, and on our bus rides. This night would be no different.

None of us wanted to sleep, for if we slept, we would be that much closer to saying goodbye.

Callie left first. We walked her down to the street where her Uber was waiting to take her to the airport. It was three o'clock in the morning and tears were already rushing down my cheeks.

In a few more hours, Aubrey would do the same.

My eyes were swollen as I walked to the all-too-familiar bus stop to catch a marshrutka to Zhytomyr. I felt hollow, knowing the comfort and joy of having my two best friends with me was now far away. We started this journey to Ukraine together in 2018. We were naive as we navigated a small Ukrainian village and were exposed to Ukrainian culture for the first time. We returned to that small village together in 2019, feeling gratitude to God for bringing us back together and giving us a new perspective on Ukraine. We met again in 2020, traveling to new parts of Ukraine and building the blocks of our friendship stronger than before.

My story with Ukraine wouldn't have been possible without a girl from the suburbs of Virginia and a girl from a small town in Nevada. They supported me when I was doubtful, they held me up when I was in pain, and they gave me a push to go exactly where I was meant to go.

SWEPT BY BUSYNESS

I signed up for a two-week intensive Ukrainian language course in Lviv from January 5–18, something I wish I would've attended before I arrived in Ukraine in August. I had one night in my apartment alone for the first time since going home and having Aubrey and Callie visit. The following day I would take another bus and return to Lviv.

I was eager to finally buckle down and study for the next two weeks. I wasn't proud of my obvious and excuse-ridden lack of commitment to studying Ukrainian since my arrival. While I did meet with Iryna frequently, language learning and studying were the first things to be pushed aside when everyday life got too busy.

I arrived in Lviv, exhausted from a six-hour bus ride from Zhytomyr. I crashed at my friends' Airbnb for the night. For the next two weeks, I arranged to stay with different Ukrainian friends in their homes so that I would be in an immersive setting and speak Ukrainian outside of class.

I didn't realize how exhausted I was until I finished the first day of class. At the start of the day, I was so excited to experience the feeling of going back to school, even if it was just for two weeks. I was surrounded by other Fulbrighters and happy that we could all be in the same city. I was back in the place where my journey with Ukraine began, a place filled with experiences that motivated me to pursue a Fulbright.

It went downhill quickly; my enthusiasm turned to bitterness and pessimism with each passing day. My teacher was belittling and lacked patience. The pace of the class was far too quick for me as a beginner. The days were long, my energy was low, and I wasn't having the experience I set out to have.

After three hours of class each morning, we ate lunch together and then went on a "cultural immersion," which included visiting different sites, museums, and events. It was three or four o'clock in the afternoon when we finished. I wanted to rest, and by the time I felt reenergized, it was time for dinner. After dinner, we wanted to spend time with one another since we knew we would return to our respective host cities soon. It would be ten o'clock at night before I even thought of starting my homework or studying, plus I still had a thirty-minute commute to my Ukrainian friends' places.

Rinse and repeat, rinse and repeat.

I wanted to do too much every day. I wanted to participate in classes. I wanted to study and do my homework. I wanted to visit sites in Lviv that I hadn't seen before. I wanted to meet Ukrainian friends for coffee. I wanted to spend quality time with my Fulbright friends. I wanted to have fun. I wanted to spend the nights with my local friends and show them how much I had learned since my first summer in Ukraine. I wanted to travel on the weekends. I wanted to do it all.

The same narrative was repeating itself. Even though I was participating in an intensive language course, language learning was still the first thing to be pushed aside when everyday life got too busy. I was swept away by busyness, and in the process, I had become a walking hypocrite. I said I wanted to do one thing, but my actions showed otherwise.

I want to tell you that I figured it out and discovered the magical balance I was seeking, a balance where I could study, explore, nurture relationships, and travel all at once. I found just the opposite. The more I tried to control and squeeze everything into my days, the more stressed I became. Maybe the answer is simple: we need to just quiet our hearts, slow down, and forget about our plans. Only then can we open ourselves up to what really matters.

GOOD TIDINGS

Amid my many struggles during the intensive Ukrainian language camp, one person deserves her own story: Olya.

Olya was one of my students from the summer camp I taught at in 2019. One day after class, she stayed late while I was organizing the classroom. We had a heart-to-heart discussion, speaking of our faith and our health struggles. I had been battling a chronic stomach illness for a year at that point and so had she. It was comforting to have someone who understood that pain.

We spent the summer getting to know each other and walking through the forest that surrounded our camp. When I returned to Lviv in August before my Fulbright orientation, Olya welcomed me to her village. It was my first time in a Ukrainian village beside the one where I taught English. There were cows, chickens, gardens, and a sense of calmness. She and her boyfriend, Rostyslav, also one of my students, showed me all around their village, shared dinner with me, and brought me to the river. It was a magical summer day.

Many Ukrainians still follow the old calendar in which Christmas is celebrated on January 6. My language course started on January 5, Christmas Eve. Olya extended an invitation to her village to celebrate Christmas together. I didn't know if I could afford to miss a whole afternoon of studying, but when would I have an opportunity to experience an authentic Ukrainian Christmas celebration with a good friend again?

I said yes and met Olya's sister at the bus station in Lviv. We took a marshrutka together to their small village.

When I traveled to Olya's village the first time, Olya's sister had helped me find the bus and asked the driver to tell me where to get off. I reflected on how much had changed in the last five months.

We arrived at Olya's house. Snow had coated the ground; it was a white Christmas. I hugged Olya joyfully as we sat down for Christmas dinner with her family. Olya told me that it's traditional for the children in the house to check for the first star in the night sky. After the first star is seen, Christmas Eve dinner can be served.

The table was covered in twelve different dishes of food accompanied with glasses of homemade vodka. An extra place setting was set, symbolic for loved ones who had passed away. I was amazed at the care and detail that went into each dish and the honor and meaning of each tradition – and the potency of the vodka. One shot goes a long way.

I was overjoyed being with Olya and her family, especially since I was so far away from mine. After dinner, Olya and I went to Mass together. The church was lit only by candles; it was ethereal. After Mass, we walked past the cemetery, which was also filled with hundreds of lit candles. Each candle was for the relatives and friends who had passed away. What a beautiful way to remember loved ones during the holidays.

When we returned to her house, she told me to wait; children singing Christmas carols would soon arrive at the door. Sure enough, a few minutes later, a group of children knocked on the door. I couldn't stop smiling. I thought caroling only happened like that in Christmas movies. Olya's mother handed them money, another Christmas tradition. For the next hour, carolers came and went, bringing Christmas joy and melodies with them.

I don't know where Olya slept the first time I visited her, nor this time. She selflessly offered me her bed to sleep in both times I visited so I would have a private place to rest. I insisted that she should sleep there, but Ukrainians always win with their hospitality. Christmas Eve in a Ukrainian village was an experience I would never forget.

It was Christmas morning. Olya and I drank coffee and ate leftover desserts for breakfast. She showed me the way to the bus stop where I could catch a bus to Lviv for my morning Ukrainian lesson. I hugged her tightly, wishing her a Merry Christmas and thanking her for one of the most wonderful evenings.

Olya and I would meet again in the coming days. She had a flat in Lviv, since she was studying there. She welcomed me to stay with her so I could practice my Ukrainian. I stayed for two nights. We didn't practice Ukrainian, but we ate cheesecake and stayed up late reminiscing. Olya was going back to her village for a few days, but she gave me an extra set of keys for her apartment so I could sleep there for the next few nights.

I can't think of a purer and more hospitable friendship than the one I shared with Olya: a young woman of faith, humility, and trust in the Lord. She inspired me with her kindness and openness, a kind of love that I hope to extend to others.

A COLORFUL CELEBRATION

There is a tradition of celebrating the "Old New Year" in Ukraine on January 14. In some parts of the country, Ukrainians celebrate this day with a festival called "Malanka." Sydney had learned about it in her host city,

Chernivtsi, a city about 175 miles southeast of Lviv known for its Malanka festivities.

What I loved about Sydney was that she wasn't a surface traveler; she was always seeking unique travel experiences. When she asked me if I wanted to come to Chernivtsi for the Malanka carnival, I couldn't say yes fast enough.

If there were ever two people who could battle for the best budget travel hacks, Sydney and I would be a tag team. I loved that about her. She understood my travel style and I understood hers. We would rather take a longer train ride or Couchsurf if it meant we could save a buck to extend our future travels.

We sat on an express train from Lviv to Chernivtsi on the evening of Saturday, January 11. That weekend would kick off the Malanka festivities. I felt good about going to Malanka; I wouldn't be missing any Ukrainian classes and it was an opportunity to learn more about Ukrainian culture.

We arrived at Sydney's studio apartment near midnight. We drank tea, chatted, and called it a night. Train travel in Ukraine had a way of draining a traveler, but the excitement of being in a new city was no match for the exhaustion. I drifted to sleep with anticipation of the following morning: we would explore Chernivtsi and attend a Malanka parade.

There were floats and paper mache creations, colorful costumes and folk dances, politically incorrect displays and loud music from different countries, food, and concerts. It was the strangest, coolest, jaw-dropping cultural experience I had in Ukraine. The streets were filled from the morning until the evening. Each corner brought a new surprise: a masked person, a crowd of locals celebrating, or a row of vendors selling food and souvenirs. Sydney and I were speechless, glancing at each other throughout the day with excitement and confusion.

I was thankful. Having experienced Malanka was one of those moments that confirmed my desire to travel. Days like that are why I kept pushing myself time and time again.

The celebratory day had come to a close for Sydney and me. We did what two budget travelers did to save time and money: we booked an overnight train to Lviv to arrive in time for our Ukrainian language class on Monday morning – two dedicated students. (Sydney, I hope you laugh when you read that.)

Our train left on Sunday evening at midnight. After a day of fun and adventure, it was a feat to stay awake until then. We found our bunk beds on the quiet train; Sydney had the top bunk and I had the bottom.

My ears rang and my head throbbed. Sydney clocked me in the head while struggling to fit the sheets on the top bunk. We laughed at one another. I would rather have a bump on my head than sleep on the top bunk. She was a good friend.

At four o'clock in the morning, my alarm vibrated. Shortly after, the conductor handed us our train stubs in the darkness of the cabin. We took the sheets off our bed and grabbed our bags as the train slowed to a halt. We didn't speak as we walked to the end of the wagon to exit the train.

We arrived at our Airbnb, where our Fulbright group was peacefully sleeping. Sydney and I crashed on the couch. Morning would come as if we never left.

A BET WITH AN ANGEL

After completing our intensive Ukrainian language course in Lviv, a group of friends and I decided we would explore other cities in Western Ukraine, since we were already in this part of the country. Our trip started on January 19 and included visiting the following cities: Ivano-Frankivsk, Bukovel, Yaremche, Chernivtsi, Kamianets-Podilskyi, and Khmelnytskyi. Some friends would stay for the entire trip and others would come and go.

The first leg of our trip was from Lviv to Ivano-Frankivsk. I was traveling with two other Fulbrighters, one of whom was placed in the city we were visiting. We were exhausted from our language camp, tired of living out of the same bags for three weeks, and we were letting the dreariness of winters in Ukraine get us down.

It's a recipe for negativity when you travel tired, especially with a group. It's easy to turn your tiredness into anger and impatience when something doesn't go accordingly or when someone says something that wouldn't normally rub you the wrong way. It's even more difficult to travel positively when something deeper than that tiredness is bothering you.

Around dinnertime, we arrived in Ivano-Frankivsk even more tired and now hungry. We stopped at an Italian restaurant and ate the usual "Ukrainianized" version of pasta, a mushy mix of pasta and other ingredients that aren't typically included in traditional Italian dishes. We walked down the main street, which was still lit up with sparkling lights for Christmas and New Year's. We ate cake and drank hot chocolate as our negativity slowly disappeared.

We arrived at our friend's flat, feeling much happier than we had been on the train here. We joked about our negativity and brought our attention to our friend. His experience in Ukraine hadn't been positive and he was struggling with his placement. When we met him the summer before coming to Ukraine, he seemed so happy and carefree. I knew I couldn't change his experience, but I was hoping this trip would be a reprieve for him, that he would see Ukraine differently and have fun traveling with us.

As we were getting ready for bed, we made a bet with him for the following day. We would be exploring the city in the morning, meeting another Fulbrighter, and then taking a marshrutka to our next destination. If he could stay positive for the entire day, then each of us would buy him a drink at our hotel in Bukovel. If he complained, said something negative, or focused on the downside of a situation, then he would buy us drinks.

We awoke to the greyest day that I had ever seen in Ukraine. It looked like it was going to pour or snow, and on top of that, it was freezing. He looked out the window of the flat, saying, "It's a beautiful day, isn't it?"

We laughed as we would many times that day. The things that usually beat a traveler down in Ukraine were turned into positives that day: the overcast skies, the cracks in the sidewalk that make you roll your ankle, the phlegm you have to avoid stepping on, the confusing nature of bus stations, the rudeness of marshrutka drivers, the bumpiness of unpaved roads, and the constant surprises.

Surprise after surprise, his positivity continued to impress us all. It was evening, and we finally arrived at our hotel in Bukovel. I had made the reservation for our room on my account. After booking so many accommodations for our trip, I hadn't realized that the payment for the hotel didn't process on my credit card. We were supposed to pay for it in cash upon arrival. It was 250 dollars, an amount, even combined, none of us had in Ukrainian currency.

Our friend was translating the situation from Russian to English for us when his tone changed. The woman was angry and he was translating that anger to me. The situation was heated and turned negative quickly. I recognized my shortcoming. However, the solution to the problem was simple; I just needed to go to an ATM (Bankomat).

I paid for the room in cash and met my friends upstairs, feeling the heaviness as I entered our room. I joined them on the couch, smiled, and said to my friend, "Now's a good time for you to buy us those drinks."

BATTLE WITH POSITIVITY

As much as I wished I could improve my friend's experience in Ukraine, it wasn't up to me. I could be as supportive of a friend as I could be, but ultimately it's up to the individual to make a change as he or she sees fit.

I wasn't positive in every moment during my time in Ukraine and I didn't expect my friend to be either. Life in Ukraine can be and is difficult in many ways (the word difficult is relative depending on your expectations of Ukraine and personal upbringing). In my experience, Ukraine can and will beat you down if you let it, and it will do so in full force.

If you aren't open to constant surprises, to living differently and being challenged by that, to accepting a different standard and customs than the ones you are used to, and to letting go of what you think Ukraine should be, then you will be crushed.

I held onto each of these areas with a tight grip in the beginning, and I was crushed. I believed I could control every experience I had in Ukraine. I would find a picture-perfect apartment, seamlessly mold into my role as a teaching assistant at a foreign university, create extracurricular clubs that filled entire lecture halls, and travel across the country with ease and openness.

When I held onto that grip, I was walking through each experience in Ukraine with tinted glasses. I experienced life through the lens of what I thought Ukraine should be, and when it didn't live up to my standards, I reacted negatively. When that negativity hit me, I couldn't move forward.

In those moments, I despised Ukraine. I despised the hacking and coughing of men on the streets, the snot-rockets that sprayed across the bumpy pavement, the corruption and lack of planning in many critical areas, and the feeling of disorder.

In those moments, I allowed my negative reaction to define Ukraine, my experience, and my happiness. I didn't want to live my life like that in America, in Ukraine, or anywhere in the world.

I changed. I let go of this desire to fix Ukraine and replaced it with a change in my thinking, a change towards positivity. I allowed myself to take a step back and witness Ukraine for what it was without trying to change it. This didn't mean that I never complained or that I wanted the standard of life to stay as it was in Ukraine, that I believed Ukraine shouldn't work towards positive change and reform or that everything would automatically become easy.

It meant that I could appreciate a different side of what makes Ukraine the country it is. It meant that I could open myself up to my colleagues and community even if I had to insert myself into their lives, ask them if I could join their activities, and have the same conversation 100 times over before moving forward in a meaningful relationship. It meant that I could witness Ukrainian hospitality through coffee, chocolate, and gifts, and try to return that hospitality in small ways by sharing my own culture and background. It meant that I could travel and see new parts of Ukraine and simply tell others about my experiences of those places. It meant that I could support Ukraine without being crushed by my expectation of what I thought it should be.

There are times when every traveler will wonder why they ventured to the country they did, why they chose to spend so much time in a place that they knew would be difficult to adjust to, and why they chose to leave the familiarity of their home country. How we choose to frame our experiences gives us the answers to these questions.

A HELPING HAND

I took a trip to the Carpathian Mountains in the summer of 2018. It was only a day trip, and I knew I wanted to return one day.

That day came two years later in January with a group of Fulbright friends. We had been visiting a friend in the western city of Ivano-Frankivsk and planned to take a marshrutka to the ski resort of Bukovel. While you already know about our hotel saga when we arrived, I want to tell you a story of our journey there.

We arrived at the bus station in Ivano-Frankivsk in hopes of hopping on the next bus to Bukovel but were prepared to wait. Luckily there was a bus leaving within the hour. We didn't want to wait on board since we would be sitting there for the next two hours, so we made our way to the waiting hall inside the station.

Fifteen minutes before our departure, we walked to our bus. To our surprise, it was almost full. We took the only empty seats, one in the front, one in the back, and two in the middle.

Thanks to my recurring motion sickness, my friends let me sit in the seat closest to the front. Shortly, we began our way over bumpy, unkempt city roads. I held back waves of nausea as the roads turned into winding paths between small mountain villages.

With each stop, the bus became more and more crowded until there was only standing room available. I was ready to offer my seat to an older passenger when a mother with three children boarded the already crowded bus. The next thing I knew, her two older children were happily sitting on my lap.

The younger boy looked to be about one or two years old, and the older girl was a toddler. I held both of them as the bus drove around each winding turn. They looked out the window at the snowy landscape, and I did the same. What an image: an American holding two Ukrainian children on a marshrutka. I wondered if they realized that I was a stranger who wasn't from the same country they were.

I thought about the mother whom I didn't see. She trusted the strangers on the bus. So often when we travel to a new place, there is a deep fear in trusting strangers, as I experienced when Couchsurfing, a fear that they are too different from us, a fear that the worst will happen. At that moment, I again felt what it meant to look past those fears.

The bus stopped. I looked behind me at a young woman with a baby in her arms. She said, "Дякую," a simple thank you in Ukrainian.

I smiled as we returned to the winding mountain roads.

HILLS OF COURAGE

During high school, I had spent winters learning how to snowboard. I would take a few lessons every season and hit the slopes for two- or three-day trips. I stuck to the easy and intermediate slopes where I could control my speed. It was fun, even if I would never be the best.

As the years went on, my winter snowboarding trips were replaced with college finals and weekends home to see family and friends. The more time I spent away from snowboarding, the more distant it became.

Six years later, I sat on a rusted chair lift in the mountains of Bukovel. My fifteen-dollar rental snowboard was hanging from one foot. I looked at the snowy scene painted before me. The landscape reminded me of those weekends spent snowboarding in high school. I was proud that I had the confidence to return to a happy pastime, but the steeper we ascended, the more fear began to settle within me. *Would I remember how to snowboard? What if the signs were in Ukrainian and I couldn't understand? What if we took a wrong turn and I ended up on a steep slope like the ones I used to avoid?*

Sydney and Amelia, my two friends who I had Couchsurfed with months ago, sat in the two-seater chairlift behind me. I looked back and waved at them, wondering if they had similar thoughts. We had already accomplished the feat of finding the poorly labeled ski resort and navigating equipment rental with our limited language skills. I tried to remind myself that the hard part was over. Now it was time to have fun.

We met at the top of the mountain after gliding off the chairlift. Unfortunately, Sydney had experienced the same fears I had, and she decided to take the lift back down. It was me, Amelia, and a big beautiful mountain range waiting to be explored.

I strapped my other foot onto my snowboard and told Amelia, a skier, that I'd meet her at the bottom if we lost sight of one another. She went first and I followed her lead.

It was like riding a bike, you never forget. As I picked up speed, the same feeling I had when I used to snowboard came back. It was even better this time. The wind blew on my face, and the view of the pine trees and surrounding mountains erased the fears that seemed so far away now. I was snowboarding in the mountains of Ukraine.

I met my friend at the bottom of the mountain. Her smile was bigger than mine as she shouted, "You did it, Kat!"

She was right; I did it. Our day continued just like that. We went from trail to trail, working our way down slopes my high school self would never have attempted. Every time we made our way down a black trail, my friend was waiting at the bottom, ready to say, "You did it, Kat!"

As dusk began to settle, we returned our rentals. I hugged my friend and thanked her for a day that I'd always remember. It was a day of more than just mountains and snowboarding. It was a day of having courage and realizing the gift of a friend who will give you a boost just when you need it most.

PICTURE-PERFECT

High on life and high on adventure. We snowboarded on each mountain, making runs for two hours before having a break and getting back at it. We laughed and told stories on the chairlift to the top. We joked that Ukrainians ski just like they drive. I'll let you decide what that means.

It was a picture-perfect day, a day that started with fear and ended with confidence. I wanted to do it all over again. I wanted to spend more time in the mountains.

I wished we were there for one more night, just one more night to have an extra day of snowboarding and fun. Our trip to Bukovel was a two-night stay: we arrived in the evening on the first night and snowboarded early the next day. The mountains were getting icier, and the air was bitter cold. We had ourselves a fun day of adventure, but it was time to call it quits.

Amelia headed back to the hotel to relax and read before dinner. That sounded peaceful, but I had other plans. I met our other friend at the bottom of the mountain, returned my gear, and headed to our next destination.

The woman behind the front desk handed us our wristbands and robes. My friend went to the men's locker room, and I made my way to the women's locker room. I peeled off layers of thermals, my sports bra, and wool socks. I rinsed off in the shower, feeling the stiffness in my body from my tired muscles. I put on my robe and walked to the mirror, pulling my wet curls into a tight bun at the nape of my neck. I walked back to my locker and slipped my bikini on. I passed the mirror one more time before opening the door.

I didn't think the day could get any better. It was magical. Lounge chairs surrounded a jetted pool with a bar in the center. There were saunas of all kinds, a salt room, and a heated pool outside, with the mountains surrounding each side.

We swam through the bar area into the outdoor pool. I swam in a circle, admiring the mountains from each side. I was just on the top of those mountains. The view from below was just as majestic.

I was completely immersed in the view when I felt two hands grab my waist from behind me. The cold air hit my shoulders, then my arms, and then my bare stomach. I landed a few feet away, relieved to feel the warmth of the water as my body submerged to the bottom.

I splashed him as payback for throwing me and disturbing my peaceful and reflective moment. Yet, I was smiling, thinking of moments spent at the Jersey Shore where my brothers and guy friends would take turns throwing us over the crashing waves, sometimes making it over the wave and other times body surfing to the shoreline.

The hot air wrapped around my body, soothing my achiness. We tested every sauna, spending ten minutes inside followed by an ice-cold shower. Hot, then cold, hot, then cold.

The windows were glass from floor to ceiling. We stood on the second-floor level, wrapped in our robes, admiring the same view but from a higher point.

Our time at the spa was up. We returned to our respective

locker rooms. I looked in the mirror again. I was content, I was happy, and I was proud of the woman in the mirror.

NO PLACE TO REST

After visiting the western mountain towns of Bukovel and Yaremche, Amelia departed to her host city, Ivano-Frankivsk, and the three of us continued to Chernivtsi. Since I was only in Chernivtsi for a day to celebrate Malanka a week prior, Sydney generously invited us back to her host city to explore more.

It was the last weekend in January. All of us had been traveling for almost six weeks. Train after train, bus after bus, plane after plane.

Grayson had booked a hostel in advance as Sydney's apartment was small and could only sleep two people unless someone wanted to sleep on the floor. He checked into his hostel down the block from Sydney's flat while I accompanied Sydney. I set my bags down near her front door.

It was late afternoon, and I could see the exhaustion on Sydney's face. I knew that exhaustion all too well. It was the traveler's enemy – a sign that burnout was near. Sydney needed a break.

"Are you sure you're up for hosting me tonight?" I asked.

She reassured me that it was okay; she would have more energy tomorrow. As the evening drew near, Sydney asked me if I would mind getting a room in the hostel where Grayson was staying. I held no anger towards my friend. There were many times when I let people down because

I needed to press pause, and there would continue to be times like that.

I tossed my backpack over my shoulder, hugged Sydney, and walked to the hostel. We would meet again in the morning. I wasn't the slightest bit angry at my friend, yet there was one thing I was disappointed about as I entered the twelve-person mixed dorm room: for the cost of our two beds, Grayson and I could've gotten a quiet, two-bedroom Airbnb.

It was strange to wander around Chernivtsi that evening without Sydney. It was Sydney's host city after all. Grayson and I went to a cafe for our evening tea, a tradition we had both gotten used to since living in Ukraine.

We walked along the main pedestrian street, looping our way back to our hostel as our conversation dissipated into laughter.

I laid in my bottom bunk bed and Grayson laid in his. The dorm was surprisingly quiet, a sign of the "off-season" and the cold winter. We texted each other so as not to wake up our neighbors. However, our laughs probably kept them up anyway. I heard Grayson laugh again before falling asleep.

Sydney needed time to herself and we respected her. Grayson and I were on our own again for the morning. We visited a new cafe and read books on our Kindles. Although it wasn't the evening and morning we had anticipated in Chernivtsi, I think we both enjoyed the slowness and ease of a good coffee on a grey winter morning.

When we finally met up with Sydney, she appeared happier and lighter as she showed us her host city: we visited her university, which was a UNESCO site, met her colleague, and weaved through the cobblestone streets. Sometimes travel plans don't go according to plan, but if you're lucky, you still have good friends by your side.

AN ACCIDENTAL FIRST

It was the end of January in Ukraine and we were nearing the end of our Western winter trip. Each day brought us grey skies and cold temperatures. It would have been more comfortable to stay warm indoors, but we were determined to continue seeing new parts of Ukraine.

Sydney and I sat in an empty restaurant on January 24, the only tourists exploring a summer-friendly destination: an ancient castle in Kamianets-Podilskyi, one of the last destinations on our Western Ukraine trip. Grayson had returned to Kramatorsk.

We saw the beautiful remnants of the castle, albeit at the expense of our cold hands and runny noses. After our visit, we ate a traditional Ukrainian lunch and talked about our travel plans for the next day. We would be heading sixty miles to Khmelnytskyi, the final destination on our self-made Western Ukrainian tour.

The previous night, we had looked up possible transportation routes, checking train, bus, and ridesharing websites, including BlaBlaCar: an app where you can pay to join someone's car ride. We searched on our respective accounts, laughing as her account was accidentally set to Spanish and mine was set to Hindi. We weighed our options and decided not to take BlaBlaCar because we didn't want to be tied to someone else's schedule. If we took the bus that left once an hour, we would have flexibility in our day.

As we continued eating and discussing our upcoming adventure, Sydney checked her phone. She looked up at me with a glimpse of confusion.

"What does this say?" she asked.

I looked at her phone. She had an email from BlaBlaCar, written in Spanish. I looked up at her and burst into laughter. When I caught my breath, I relayed the message: we were scheduled to take a BlaBlaCar from Kamianets-Podilskyi to Khmelnytskyi the following day at two o'clock in the afternoon.

That's the funny thing about traveling: no matter how much you try to plan, there are always changes. Here we were in an empty Ukrainian restaurant laughing to ourselves over my friend's accidental reservation. We laughed even harder as we considered which language we should respond in: Spanish, Hindi, English, Ukrainian, or Russian. The next day, we hopped in the BlaBlaCar, looked at each other in the backseat, and smiled. After all the planning we did, my friend's mistake allowed us to try something new, deepen our trust in strangers, and learn to laugh along the way.

Пока, Пока

After six weeks of travel to the United States and across Western Ukraine, I needed a break from the go-go-go. I wanted to sleep in my bed, eat a home-cooked meal, and see familiar streets.

I arrived back in Zhytomyr on January 26. It felt good to be in my home city after many travels, but I had another motive for being back in Zhytomyr.

My best friend was leaving.

I met Natasha in October at the university where I taught. She was completing her Master's degree there. I had begun to settle into my chaotic teaching routine, becoming more comfortable with my colleagues and more confident in my responsibilities and lesson plans.

In my department, there were about ten women I taught with. Some women were older, in their fifties or sixties, some were middle-aged, and others were younger. I connected with each of them in their own ways, but I missed working directly with colleagues who were my age.

Maybe God heard my longing, because one day, a new secretary appeared in our department. In the United States, we'd call her job "work-study," but they called her a secretary. She was a Zhytomyr native who was in her final semester for her Master's degree, and she happened to be my age. She was shy when it came to speaking English, but not shy in asking me to go out for coffee.

I usually had a twenty-minute break between classes and an hour-and-twenty-minute break if I didn't have back-to-back classes. We spent those breaks getting to know each other, drinking coffee, talking about boys, dreaming of travel plans, and becoming friends.

To say I was grateful for our friendship would be an understatement. Around Natasha, I didn't just feel like the American, and in turn, I didn't just feel like she was another Ukrainian. Our friendship wasn't situational; whether we had met in the United States or Ukraine, I'm confident our friendship would've blossomed.

We met outside of school too. We ate sushi together, went shopping together, and walked around the city together. She'd help me with my Ukrainian studies and buying bus tickets, laughing at my travel stories in the process, and I'd help her with English studies. She helped me pick out Ukrainian gifts for my family back home, and I helped her pick out an outfit for her graduation. To have a friend like her in my host city was one of my greatest joys.

At the end of the semester in December, Natasha graduated from her program. I was proud of her, but sad knowing that she would no longer be working in our department. My sadness went beyond that. Natasha would be leaving to work on a six-month cruise around the world starting in February.

This would be the last time we saw each other. We had hope that we would meet in the summer months if I extended my stay and she returned, but that was uncertain. We agreed to meet for coffee to say goodbye, a symbol of how our friendship began. We took a picture together in the city center, and she walked me back to my apartment. We stood on the corner of the busy market street, hugging each other tightly. A tear rolled off my cheek as I wished her the best of luck on her new adventure. I was looking into a mirror as a tear rolled off her cheek, as she too wished me well in Zhytomyr. It wouldn't be the same without her.

"God bless you," she said as we let go. God had already blessed me with the gift of a friend like her.

INTERNAL BATTLE

I was happy to be in Zhytomyr for a few days to recoup but soon realized that this precious free time off from teaching was an opportunity for me to see different cultures and cities. After a four-day break, I thought I was ready to go again.

"Do you want to go to Moldova for a few days?" Sydney's text read.

Sydney and I clicked. We worked well together when traveling – seeking authentic experiences, willing to take risks and make mistakes, and happy with the simplicity of budget travel. I admired her travel style. Like me, she had study abroad and travel experience, but she was never over-confident. Rather, she was humble and open to what each new place would offer.

It was January 28. I felt sad that night, still ruminating on Natasha's departure. The Uber soon arrived at an unfamiliar bus station in Kyiv at 10:30 at night. I thanked the driver and walked into the station, cognizant of my surroundings. I found the ticket stand and mentally prepared myself to be yelled at as usual. After almost six months of getting yelled at by Ukrainian bus drivers and cashiers, I could handle it again tonight.

I got yelled at, didn't know which platform my bus was leaving from, and gave up. I didn't have the energy to keep going; Ukraine won.

My bus was leaving at eleven o'clock. I sat on a bench outside the station and texted Sydney to tell her apologetically that I didn't think I could travel; something didn't feel right. After messaging her, I looked up Airbnbs in Kyiv. Nobody would know I was here. I could escape from the busyness and have a quiet staycation in Kyiv instead of taking a ten-hour overnight bus to Chisinau, the capital of Moldova.

The clock was nearing eleven. I saw a bus pass me with a sign that read, "Кишинів."

"Damnit," I mumbled as my decision to go or stay became more difficult now that I found my bus.

I showed my ticket to the driver and took my seat for the next ten hours. As soon as I sat down, my sadness turned into silent tears. I was exhausted. I felt sad, knowing I lost a friend in Zhytomyr who made my experience there so fruitful. I felt guilty: traveling the world, knowing my father just celebrated his ninety-fifth birthday, 4600 miles away from me. I felt like I was losing myself in this constant wave of busyness, in this constant need to prove something through my travels and daily choices.

A man pointed to the seat next to me. I stood up and tried to wipe my tears away quickly as he took his place on the bus. He turned to me, asking for a pen. I could understand this simple question in Ukrainian and handed him the pen wedged in the pages of my journal.

He continued to speak to me, our conversation becoming too advanced for my beginner knowledge. I told him I was American and didn't understand. He smiled and thanked me for the pen.

My tears dried as I was lulled to sleep by the moving bus. We were well on our way to Chisinau. I had never cried so much over a simple choice – whether to get on a bus or not. Traveling was one of the biggest joys in my life, and I had the opportunity to do it every weekend if I chose to. *Why couldn't I shake my sadness?*

In the coming weeks, I would endure pain from this internal battle: to travel or to live intentionally, slowly, and according to my values.

It wasn't traveling that made me cry that night. It was the knowledge that while I was traveling, I was giving up time I could use to write letters to my father, call family members and friends, exercise and run, prepare healthy meals, spend time in prayer, and nurture relationships in Zhytomyr. It was the knowledge that while I chose to stay in Zhytomyr, I was giving up the thrill of meeting new people from different cities and countries, the joy of exploration and discoveries, the inspiration to write, and the desire I had to keep pushing myself.

A traveler's dilemma – to stay or to go.

GUARDIAN

Five hours were behind me. Five more to go. It was four o'clock in the morning when the bus stopped. I was half-asleep as I looked through the front windshield. The road had turned from paved gravel to dirt. There was a building on my left and one on my right, and a gate in front of us. I looked at the other passengers on the bus; all of us expressed the same grogginess and confusion.

We were at the checkpoint into Moldova, or so I thought. When I booked my ticket, I assumed there was one checkpoint and that this was it: Ukraine to Moldova. Chisinau would be another two hours away.

I tried to check Google Maps to see my location, but I had no phone service. The bus ride was supposed to be ten hours long. I didn't understand how we could be at the border already.

A border guard with a Ukrainian emblem boarded the bus and collected our passports. After ten minutes, we were ushered off the bus and told to take our belongings with us. I made eye contact with my neighbor who had asked me for the pen a few hours earlier. He pointed to the building on our left. I had traveled through country borders in the past, but I never experienced this.

We were directed into a dark room. I followed the crowd and took my place in the pitch darkness. I was nervous but too tired to give attention to my fear. We stood in pitch blackness for two or three minutes before the lights came on.

The floors of the run-down building were made of concrete, showing cracks in many places. Stray dogs were wandering through the room. I could see my neighbor on the other side. He nodded and smiled.

After thirty minutes, we were allowed back onto the bus. I was relieved to be able to go back to sleep. Shortly after, the same border guard entered the bus again. He called out, "Катерина!" meaning Catherine in English.

I sat in my place, waiting for someone to respond. Катерина was a common name in Ukraine.

He shouted louder, "Американська дівчина!"

My full name is Kathleen, or "Катерина," the closest transliteration in the Ukrainian language. I was the American girl that the guard was calling.

I looked at my neighbor again. I didn't like the idea of following the guard at 4:30 in the morning into another dark room, but I had no choice if I wanted to make it to Chisinau. He led me to the building on the right this time. I stood in front of four guards, my fear mounting. *What if the bus left without me? What if I was stuck here alone?*

I spoke first, telling them in Ukrainian that I couldn't understand Russian or Ukrainian languages. They waved my passport in the air and spoke firmly as they pointed to my Ukrainian visa, which had expired two months prior.

When the border guard initially came onto the bus, he just asked for our passports. I gave him my passport, but I didn't give him my Ukrainian residence card, a card that replaced my expired visa and allowed me to legally live in Ukraine for the next four years.

I dug through my backpack as quickly as possible and handed them the residence card, my hands shaking all the while. They glared at me. Annoyance was written on their faces. I walked back to the bus with my passport and residence card in hand. I sat in my seat, my neighbor smiling at my safe return.

PASSPORT ROULETTE

Moldova was a wild ride, and it was just day one. After an overnight bus, I was solo, groggy, and off-guard. I walked forty minutes to the hostel, listening to a mix of Russian and Romanian by passersby and reading signs that looked like Italian. I could understand the signs, having lived in Italy for a year, but to hear Romanian was confusing, mixes of what sounded like both Slavic and Romance languages.

I stopped for a coffee and continued on my way to the hostel, where I met Sydney.

"Sydney, I don't know what happened last night." I couldn't get the words out fast enough.

I told her of my border adventures. I was mistaken; I had assumed I would have to go through one border crossing from Ukraine to Moldova.

After being questioned for my residence permit at the Ukrainian border, the bus pulled up to a second border fifty feet ahead of us. The same drill was repeated, although this time I just needed to give my passport to the Moldovan guard.

My passport was returned without any problems this time. I drifted to sleep, thankful to get a few more hours of rest before arriving in Chisinau. Here's where I went wrong.

A half-hour later, the same story repeated itself.

A half-hour later, the same story repeated itself.

A half-hour later, the same story repeated itself.

A half-hour later, the same story repeated itself.

Six border crossings to get from Kyiv to Chisinau on an overnight bus. Out of Ukraine, into Moldova, out of Moldova, into the autonomous territory of Transnistria, out of Transnistria, and into Moldova. There was no sleeping, just a whole lot of confusion and a whole lot of border guards.

"You went through Transnistria by yourself!" Sydney shouted.

At the time, I didn't realize I had entered the autonomous part of the country. I was advised not to travel through this territory by myself. This breakaway region is not controlled by the central government and there is limited U.S. emergency aid to American citizens there. I booked an overnight bus with the start destination as Kyiv and the end as Chisinau; the exact route wasn't listed.

Sydney and I laughed together and drank sea buckthorn tea, telling our adventures and stories of our journeys to get here. Over the next few days, we explored the capital, met new travel friends, visited ancient monasteries, and ended our trip in Tiraspol, a city in Transnistria, this time with friends and a plan.

Since this is a book about Ukraine, I won't write about the

details of Moldova. I will only say that being in Tiraspol felt like being warped in time – stuck in a place I didn't want to be stuck.

OCCUPIED

We wanted to visit Tiraspol to see our friend Isaac, a Fulbrighter who was placed there, a Fulbrighter who also happened to be Sydney's boyfriend. Sydney had already been to Tiraspol before to visit him. I'm not sure we would've been in Moldova if it wasn't for her Fulbright romance, but I was thankful for an opportunity to visit a new place with two good friends.

Make that three good friends; another Ukrainian Fulbrighter joined our trip, Lilly. The four of us met up and explored the time capsule city, thankful for one another's presence amid the dreary winter days.

It was Sunday, February 2, and our time exploring the city was coming to a close. Our "visas" would end at midnight, and by visa, I mean a little square paper that allowed us to stay in Transnistria for three days.

Lilly and I said goodbye to Sydney and Isaac, who were on their way back to Chisinau. Lilly and I would be taking a bus back to Ukraine.

We arrived at the bus station in Tiraspol. Isaac had lent us money all weekend, and we paid him on Venmo in return. In Transnistria, foreign bank and credit cards don't work. There's no way to get money from an ATM without a local bank card. You either have to borrow Transnistrian rubles from someone or convert currency.

Isaac had given us enough money to cover our inexpensive bus ride back to Ukraine. We walked to the cashier and asked for two bus tickets to Odesa.

The cashier informed us that the bus was sold out and that there were no other buses to Odesa for the day.

Lilly and I looked at each other in shock. We only had enough Transnistrian rubles for two bus tickets and some pocket change in Ukrainian currency. We thought about staying the night and catching the same bus the next day but realized again that we didn't have enough money, and our visas would expire.

We were stuck.

As we exited the bus station, we were bombarded by taxi drivers and a woman who offered to drive us for free to the border. Overwhelmed, Lilly and I walked away from the station, passing a currency exchange window.

As we passed the currency exchange window, I remembered I had a fifty-dollar bill in the back of my passport case for travel emergencies.

"Lilly, I have money!" I said, relieved we had a way to return to Ukraine.

We walked back to the mosh of shouting taxi drivers and haggled with one who agreed to drive us across the Moldovan-Ukrainian border and two and a half hours to Odesa.

The familiar Ukrainian landscape and villages came into view. I was fifty dollars poorer, but 100 percent happier to be back in Ukraine.

OCEAN WAVES

Lilly and I arrived in Odesa after a bumpy journey from Tiraspol. The air smelled different than Zhytomyr, the city felt fun and energizing like Kyiv, and the feeling of being in Ukraine again was comforting. Lilly was a Fulbright researcher with a home base in the ocean city of Odesa. It was still winter, but I was happy to be in a beach city visiting a friend.

I planned to stay in Odesa for one night before taking an overnight train back to Kyiv on February 3. The day we arrived in Odesa, Lilly received an email from Harvard University: she had been selected to interview for a graduate program.

With a change in plans, I asked Lilly if she wanted me to get a hostel so she could concentrate on her interview preparation. She kindly let me stay, but I wanted to respect her space.

I spent the following day exploring Odesa solo. It was oddly refreshing to be alone. The stark quietness of being alone surprised me, as I had been traveling with friends for weeks up until then. I took myself on a coffee date, I journaled, and I walked barefoot on the beach.

The waves crashed in front of me, rolling back into the dark sea before crashing again. The sand fell between my fingers, one grain at a time. The cold wind blew on my face. I was happy, taken back to summer days as a child at the beach.

I couldn't think of anyone but my brother, my sweet brother, gone too soon. He was a father-figure to me, always there for me and supporting all of my ideas, however "untraditional" they were. He would be proud that I continued to do what I loved, even through the loss and pain.

He owned a beach house down the Jersey Shore, a beautiful oceanfront house a step away from the big blue waves. Every summer, we spent days visiting the beach, losing track of time building sandcastles, playing in the waves, and collecting seashells. He hardly ever actually went to the beach, but he took great joy in welcoming us to his home and sharing lots of ice cream with me as a child.

I closed my eyes and continued to let the cold sea breeze take my mind to him. When he was diagnosed with cancer in 2014, I knew our days were limited. We would spend the next year and a half trying to squeeze in as many dinner dates and beach memories as we could, not knowing when our time together would come to an end.

It was 2016; I was in China, studying and traveling for four weeks so far. I received a call that I needed to book the next flight home from Shanghai to New York City. Numb to the world around me, I sat on that fifteen-hour plane ride, begging God to let me arrive home in time to say goodbye.

As we drove to the hospital, a rainbow appeared in the sky. My brother was a rainbow baby, a baby that comes after a miscarriage. He was waiting for me. I held his hand and whispered "I love you" as he went from this world to the next.

I was twenty years old when my brother passed away. His loss would always live with me, but so would his joy, his zest for life, his humility, and his ability to make everyone in a room feel welcomed and loved. I stood up and brushed the sand off. His memory would live within me in every corner of my heart and in every corner of wherever my next destination would be.

SPLIT DECISION

Lilly completed her Harvard interview; I was proud of her and the hardships she overcame to get to this point. I didn't know her whole story, but her perseverance and determination to continue on the path towards achieving a big dream of hers left me inspired. Spoiler alert: she's now completing her Master's degree at Harvard.

After a short trip, I asked her if I could return in the spring when it would be warmer and when we would have more time to explore together. She smiled, agreeing.

I walked to the train station, ready for my second overnight travel adventure of the week. It was hard to believe that just a few days prior, I was playing passport roulette through Moldova and Transnistria. Now, I would be taking an overnight train back to where I started: Kyiv.

Even after almost six months of travel in Ukraine, I still chose the third class option for train travel. I loved the feeling of being able to travel so inexpensively in a big open cabin with different people. What I still didn't like were top bunks, which I had that night. I swore I would never take a top bunk again, but it was the only open ticket left.

After ten long hours and 300 miles traveled, I arrived in the familiar city of Kyiv. I did what I always did; I got a cappuccino at the train station. There was something so mediocre but so satisfying about fifty-cent cappuccinos at bus and train stations in Ukraine. I wouldn't say the same in the United States, but Ukraine hooked me.

I spent the morning wandering around, drinking coffee, and buying new makeup to make myself feel more put together after weeks of traveling. I met my Fulbright friend's Ukrainian roommate, who generously gave me an extra set of keys for their apartment where I would be staying the night. I walked forty-five minutes to their apartment, not wanting to be on another form of public transportation.

A fresh cappuccino was sitting on the windowsill as the sun set behind it. I didn't realize it, but I had fallen asleep for hours. I took a sip of the coffee, grateful my Fulbright friend picked me up a fresh cup on his way home from teaching.

We went out to dinner, we read on our Kindles, we drank cider, and we had a good night together. The following morning, I woke up feeling refreshed until I remembered my travel plans. I would be taking an eighteen-hour overnight train to a city called Mariupol that night. Three overnight travel days in one week; *what was I thinking?*

I wasn't living up to my new promise to travel more intentionally and to slow down. If anything, I was doing the opposite. *What was I running away from in Zhytomyr? Why couldn't I sit in one place and be content? Why couldn't I slow down?*

I don't remember what I did that day, but I do remember this. I ripped my train ticket in half, I left my backpack unpacked, I messaged my friend in Mariupol to apologize, and I asked my friend's roommate if I could crash at their apartment for another night. (My Fulbright friend was at work during this time and, to this day, gives me crap for asking his roommate and not him if I could stay.)

I could take the crap, but I couldn't take an eighteen-hour train ride. I was done, burned out more than I ever felt while traveling: emotionally, physically, and mentally.

Change needed to happen, but it would only happen if I set boundaries for myself and aligned my actions with my words.

WAVE OF LONELINESS

Eight weeks. Eight full weeks of adventuring to new corners of the world and familiar ones, of laughing with friends who I couldn't imagine life without, of being reunited with those who will never let me fall, of getting lost in late nights that I never wanted to end, of celebrating life's little moments and of struggling through changes and growth.

Each day was new. Each day was exciting. Each day turned into a night I spent waiting in anticipation for what was to come next.

Silence.

Utter and complete silence overtook me as I arrived in my apartment, alone, on February 7. This is what I said I wanted when I ripped that ticket to Mariupol. I set down my bags. I looked around slowly, somehow expecting things to be different, but finding an odd sense of familiarity as I saw my belongings in the same place I left them. Everything was the same, yet I couldn't shake the overwhelming feeling of emptiness.

I busied myself. I unpacked my bags, did laundry, and went to the grocery store to restock my bare shelves. I answered long overdue emails and messages, I cleaned my room, and I settled in, expecting to simply mold back into the life I lived here for the last few months.

"Now what?" I whispered.

I felt so full of everything, yet so empty at the same time. I looked out the window of my balcony and couldn't fight the feeling of loneliness that had been brewing inside me. That's what I was running away from. The loneliness was calling for the laughter, the conversations, and the exploration I had experienced the last few weeks. It was calling for the freedom of not knowing what the next day held, but being so excited to live it. It was calling for companionship, for connection, for being in harmony with the ebb and flow of life on the road.

I've spent nights camping under the stars on a beach. I've had conversations that lasted until the late hours of the morning. I've journeyed through different seasons of life, of grief, and of love, but I've never journeyed to a place I didn't choose, a place where I'd live alone for nine months. To be so full one moment, and so empty the next – it's the curse and beauty of deciding to leave your home and embrace the new life you've set out, knowing that life will come with challenges, reflections, and change.

Oh, how beautiful that life is. The moments that make it all worth it, the friendships that make you believe a friendship could last forever, the laughter that fuels more laughter, the passion that ignites itself when you see a new place, and the unexpected beauty of letting go of your plan a little bit more each day. That's the fullness that makes the loneliness disappear. It makes the loneliness just another wave in this ocean, a wave that I'd ride into the next chapter of this journey, wherever it took me.

EXCHANGE

Irena's daughter, Vlada gifted me a handmade card that read, "Welcome, Kat!" The card sat in my lap as we drove through the unfamiliar streets to the dorm room where I would be staying until I found an apartment in Zhytomyr. I dug out my planner from my carry-on backpack, remembering there were stickers in the back. I peeled two stickers off the page, a heart and a smiley face, and handed them to the little girl sitting in the backseat with me.

Over the next several months, I met up with Irena, Valery, and Vlada often. We would go to the market, drink coffee, and share meals. I consider Irena, Valery, and Vlada to be my adoptive Ukrainian family, and I think they would feel the same.

Vlada was eight years old. I quickly learned that she loved arts and crafts, dancing, and stationery. The first few times we met, Vlada always gifted me a small trinket or a card. As I adjusted to a new country and city, those little gifts warmed my heart more than she realized.

Once a week, as I walked through the market or a new store, I would keep an eye out for a gift for Vlada, as I was sure to see her soon. She was only a child, but she had already learned the great art of how to make strangers feel welcome.

It was only a colorful pen or a cute notebook, maybe a sparkly keychain or a few stickers, but it was how our little relationship developed. Even though Vlada knew a few English words and I knew a few Ukrainian words, our way of communicating was through these little gifts.

I was sitting in my apartment, lonely as ever. A message from Irena lit up my phone.

"Do you want to come over today?" she asked.

I was thankful. Seeing Irena and her family was exactly what I needed. I reached into my closet and put their Christmas gifts in a tote bag. I didn't have an opportunity to give them their gifts when Aubrey and Callie had visited.

Valery picked me up from my apartment and we drove to theirs on the other side of the city. He hung my coat as I walked into their homey apartment. Vlada and Irena greeted me with hugs. I handed Vlada her gift as she smiled. I was expecting to have coffee and be in good company; I wasn't expecting this.

The entire dining room table was filled with platters of food. There wasn't a single empty space on the table. I turned toward Irena, shocked.

"I read your blog post," she said, smiling.

The day before, I had written a blog post called *Waves of Loneliness,* the previous story you read.

Vlada danced around the room, showing me all the steps she learned in her ballroom dance class since I had last seen her. She continued to dance while Valery, Irena, and I feasted on the delicious spread Irena made. Irena prepared coffee and cheesecake while Vlada and I made little shapes out of clay and baked them. She placed all of our creations in a tiny box, tied the box carefully with ribbon, and handed it to me. The box served as a symbol of a little girl with a big heart and a small family in Zhytomyr with an abundance of love, care, and hospitality.

GOING BANANAS

After six months of living in Ukraine, I became accustomed to eating chocolate and dessert a few too many times a day. In the beginning, when offered chocolate and coffee, I would politely decline, explaining that I try to only drink one coffee a day or that I was trying to be vegan. This was true for my lifestyle in America, and most Ukrainians respected me, even if they asked me three or four times if I was sure that I didn't want either before finally conceding. Truth be told, I didn't want to drink three or more coffees a day and eat sweets with each one. If I said yes to each person, I would've been in the situation I was in by February.

Nearly two months of winter vacation were coming to an end. I hadn't attended any of my fitness classes or running club outings. My jeans hugged my hips tighter than they had when I first arrived in Ukraine and I could see the effects of the extra sugar, cookies, and coffees in the roundness of my cheeks. I had given up my healthier lifestyle that I had lived in America and succumbed to Ukrainian food culture. It was easier to accept offerings, since I felt rude each time I declined hosts who generously extended their hospitality to me through coffee and gifts of chocolate.

If I was going to continue to abort my healthy eating habits with colleagues and local friends, changes had to happen in other ways. I came to a compromise: when I was in my apartment, I was going to eat healthy foods. I grabbed one of my tote bags from the kitchen and locked the door behind me. I didn't feel like fighting the lines at the big supermarket, so I decided to stop at the local market across the street. I went to the first stand I saw, which sold bananas. I looked in my wallet; I had forgotten to go to the ATM. I only had the equivalent of one dollar in change. I picked up three bananas, estimating I could buy a small bunch with that amount.

The woman behind the table told me the price. It was just over the amount I had. "Crap," I mumbled. I ripped the bunch of bananas, putting one back and handing her two. I realized my mistake as the seller began to scream at me in Russian and held up the one banana I left behind.

She was angry, shouting that no one was going to buy just one banana. I apologized, knowing full-well that I could've just gone to the ATM. As I started towards my next destination, I checked my phone and saw a memory on Facebook. I laughed to myself at the irony of the situation. This time last year, I was attending shows at New York Fashion Week. One year later, I was getting yelled at in Russian for buying two bananas instead of three.

I laughed it off and continued walking. No more excuses, I was going to sign up for a gym membership. I walked up three flights of stairs that opened into a cramped gym space with outdated equipment. The lights were off. I stood near the desk in the left corner, which I assumed was the place to sign up. I heard techno music playing from the speakers that hung from the ceiling. I waited five minutes for someone to show up while trying to understand the situation. *Was I supposed to call before I arrived? Did I have to sign-up for a membership online? Is the gym closed?*

One of the most important personal mottos I adapted in Ukraine was this: you can try to ask questions, but sometimes it's better if you don't. I jogged down three flights of stairs and walked outside past my favorite coffee stand. At least I knew where to get a good cappuccino and pastries.

ANOTHER GUARDIAN

I was still lonely and in a funk; I wanted to be around a friend of the same faith who could help me re-center. Claire was the person who could do just that. Ostroh, a town 120 miles from Zhytomyr, was the next destination on my list.

Through my many bus adventures, I found a website that listed bus routes with pictures of the actual bus – game changer. I could now book a bus and know which one to look for in the maze that is a Ukrainian bus station.

I booked a bus to Rivne, where I would then take a local marshrutka to Ostroh. The bus I picked was yellow; I couldn't miss a yellow bus.

My bus was set to depart at nine o'clock in the morning on February 12. I arrived at the familiar bus station at 8:30, giving myself plenty of time to fret and find the correct bus. As the clock neared nine, a yellow bus pulled into the lot. I double-checked the sign in the front of the bus which read, "Рівне." A yellow bus going to Rivne; it was as easy as that.

I handed my ticket to the driver, happy to have found my bus in record time. Much to my surprise, he shook his head, telling me it wasn't the correct bus.

It had to be my bus. It was yellow, matching the one in the picture on my ticket, and it was going to Rivne. I wandered around the station, frantically searching for another yellow bus, which I assumed had already left by now. It was well after the departure time; there wasn't another bus in sight that was yellow or going to Rivne.

I returned to the place I started and met the bus driver again. He assured me that my bus was yellow and that it would come soon. I thanked him as he got into the yellow bus and drove away towards his destination: Rivne.

After forty-five minutes of waiting, I succumbed to the reality that I would have to rebook a new ticket and try again later that day or the following day. Just as I was texting Claire to inform her that I missed my bus, what do you know, a yellow bus pulled into the lot.

I jogged over to the bus to read the sign in the front window: "Рівне". I handed my ticket to the driver, holding my breath as he scanned the code. He gestured me on the bus.

It was a relief to be on the correct bus to Rivne. My journey still included another bus to get to Ostroh, but I was glad to be one step closer to seeing my friend.

After a snowy bus ride, the bus pulled into the Rivne bus station. I had been here four or five times over the last few months. As I exited the bus, I was grateful to have made it this far; every successful bus ride in Ukraine was a small victory.

I wandered around the station reading different bus signs to find the correct one for Ostroh when I saw a yellow bus. The driver I met a few hours prior stood outside the bus smoking. We made eye contact. His face changed as he registered that I was the girl from Zhytomyr. He immediately smiled and nodded his head, a gesture that said, "You made it." I nodded back, a symbol of camaraderie and gratitude for Ukrainian strangers who watched over me, even through a never-ending maze of buses.

A LITTLE VILLAGE

Arriving in the western town of Ostroh was like arriving in a bigger version of Olya's village. Claire was placed in a town of 15,000 people, whereas the other Fulbrighters and myself were placed in larger cities with upwards of 150,000 people. Coming from Zhytomyr, a city with a population of 260,000 people, I couldn't help but compare my experience to Claire's.

In Ostroh, it seemed like everybody knew everybody. Claire would wave and say hello to people she knew on the way to the church, the cafe, and the university. It was small, but there was something intimate about that smallness, for with its size came community. That's what stood out to me in Ostroh.

I was coming off eight weeks of travel at this point. I gave Claire a heads up that I needed to go slowly; I couldn't run around the city seeing every attraction. I would return to Ostroh in the spring to see the things I didn't catch this time around.

Claire is a social butterfly, a determined woman who can speak to anyone and be on the move until the moment she falls asleep. I admire that about her: her ability to be a presence in a room of strangers and her perseverance to accomplish what she sets her mind to.

Ostroh was the farthest thing from a quiet little village. We were on the go from the moment I arrived until the moment I left.

On our first day in Ostroh, we got our nails done. I betrayed Irina, my nail technician in Zhytomyr. Since seeing each other in October for our conference, Claire and I compared our nails every time we met. Her nails were perfectly manicured with new designs each time. Like me, Claire also never had naked nails and had found a very talented nail artist. I told her that if the only thing we did in Ostroh was get our nails done, I'd be a happy girl.

We sat in a cozy Ukrainian house getting our nails done, arguably one of the best manicures I've ever had. I felt like a new woman when we finished. We ate cheese and drank wine before meeting Claire's church community at a local pizza restaurant. It was overwhelming for someone who doesn't like the process of meeting new people, but I was thankful that Claire welcomed me into her little part of the world.

The following day, Claire showed me the old castle. We got coffee, met her colleagues again, went out for lunch (twice), and went on a tour of the university. I was beat and I was cold. By four o'clock in the afternoon, we hadn't stopped. I asked Claire if I could borrow her keys to the apartment so I could rest while she finished the tour of the university. Claire may have had a personality full of energy, but I needed to slow down. Sometimes slowing down would mean upsetting or disappointing people, a consequence I wasn't familiar with.

The following day, we woke up at six o'clock in the morning to attend Mass at seven. I was already impressed by Claire's ability to meet new people, but I was even more impressed by her dedication to her church and faith. She attended daily Mass every morning. I could hardly stand in the back of my church in Zhytomyr once a week.

It was dark when we weaved through the back dirt roads on the way to the Polish church. The pink sun was just peeking through the darkness when we entered the cold building. I was grateful that Claire pushed me to go to Mass when my faith was so low.

Coffee in hands, Claire and I hugged tightly. I was grateful for her patience and flexibility as I adjusted to her pace and she adjusted to mine.

VALENTINE'S DAY

I didn't expect to spend Valentine's Day with this person, but life is funny like that sometimes. I was so excited to have a visitor in Zhytomyr, my first visitor since Aubrey and Callie.

This visitor was different. He had also been living in Ukraine and knew what it was like to battle with the surprises, to stay motivated, and to try to find a routine in the busyness of this chapter of our lives. I was happy to be with him, but it wasn't like I had expected.

We met up on February 14, both of us laughing at the irony of the day. I picked him up at the train station. My winter coat was soaked and I smelled of coffee. Someone had bumped into me, spilling my uncovered cup of coffee all over my jacket.

We hugged and smiled as we walked from the train station through the city, stopping to buy groceries for dinner. We could've gone out to eat, but having a home-cooked meal seemed like just the right thing for that night.

We sat in my tiny kitchen, eating tacos and drinking cider. My speaker was playing in the other room, probably with his music since he didn't like my taste. It's okay, his music was always better than mine.

To be present fully with this person, not wishing for the

past and not wanting for the future: that's what I needed. I needed to be with someone who understood me, someone who could challenge me but still understood me in a way other people couldn't, someone who made me feel like I wasn't missing anything else going on in the outside world.

He didn't seem to like my city or the cafe I took him to, my favorite cafe mind you. He seemed indifferent towards my life in Zhytomyr, but I was happy. I was happy to be with someone to try new restaurants, to walk the same paths with a new face, and to see the city through the lens of a new person.

The best part of that weekend wasn't Valentine's Day, it wasn't eating tacos, it wasn't listening to music; it was drinking together. I never drank in Zhytomyr, except for a going-home party that my colleagues threw for me. I wasn't going to drink with my students and I didn't drink alone. The night started at a bar that I had been eyeing for months. We made our way there and sat together for hours, talking about how much we missed just sitting at a bar with a good group of friends. We picked up a few more ciders on our way home, his music playing and our glasses toasting.

I said goodbye to him, a feeling of sadness for being alone again in my city and knowing that the weekend with company was over; I'd return to my daily tightrope, trying to make it across again without falling.

REASSURANCE

I walked away from the bus station. It was Sunday morning when my friend left. I walked through the market, making my way back to my apartment. I walked past the tables selling hats and gloves, the coffee truck, and the grandmas. Aside from selling food from their gardens, the grandmas also sold clothing and used goods.

It went the same way as the food: claim your space, set up a cloth, and put your goods on top. One side of the street was for selling food products and the side closest to my flat was for selling used goods. A daily garage sale.

Each morning, I would choose which side of the street I wanted to walk on. Both sides offered different products: local produce, Soviet antiques, old tools, and more.

This day brought a surprise that stopped me in my tracks.

I noticed a blue hat on a corner of a cloth where a grandma was displaying used and vintage items. The beanie had a marked letter "V" stitched onto the front. It wasn't just any letter "V"; it was the emblem of my alma mater: Villanova University.

I knew that symbol well; any Villanovan would recognize it. I stood in the middle of the sidewalk, glued in place and dumbfounded at the fact that a Villanova hat ended up on a grandma's garage sale cloth on a street corner outside my apartment in a city 4700 miles away from Villanova.

I asked her how much the hat cost as I held it in my hands, astonished.

During the previous week, I began looking for a new apartment to move into. The cockroaches and the sketchiness of the market area solidified my decision to move on. I would move into a furnished, newly renovated apartment in a different part of the city for the remaining four months of the program.

I held the hat in my hand and looked up towards the window of my balcony. The pink floral curtains made it easy to find.

This wasn't the only time I was determined to move on. After my freshman year at Villanova University, I put my deposit down to transfer to a different university called the College of William and Mary. It was the summer of 2015. I would attend a Villanova study abroad program in the Czech Republic, my first time living abroad. After the program, I would continue my studies at a new university.

Three years later, I graduated from Villanova University, and on that day, I stood in front of a crowd of students and parents giving the student commencement speech. I had worked in China for a summer, had lived in Italy for one year, and had traveled to thirty countries during that time. Had I not stayed at Villanova, I'm not sure I would have been standing on that street corner.

I placed the hat back on the cloth and thanked the grandma as I walked to my apartment. Life was messy sometimes; my life was messy at Villanova. Sometimes you think you should be somewhere else, someplace where you think you could do more or be more. I locked the door behind me and walked onto my balcony where the pink floral curtains hung. Sometimes you're right where you need to be.

INVITATION

By now, I think you've gotten the idea that travel and I have a unique relationship: travel fuels me in a way that feeds my soul. However, on the flip side, I face constant burnout from wanting to see so many places and do so many things.

I kept talking about wanting to step away from the busyness, to slow down, and to take a break. You'd think I would have stopped after two months of travel. I couldn't, not with an email like that in my inbox.

The message from the Fulbright director read, "We planned a Fulbright outreach trip to Eastern Ukraine. Would you like to join? Please let me know as soon as possible."

I ruminated on the message: a three-day trip to Eastern Ukraine from February 18–20 sponsored by the Fulbright Program.

A second message sat in my inbox from the director: "Would you also be interested in giving a fashion presentation at the Kyiv University of Design on February 17? All expenses paid."

It was Sunday, February 16 as I sat in my apartment packing for what felt like the hundredth time since mid-December. I messaged my Fulbright friend to see if I could crash at his place for the night in Kyiv. My presentation at the University of Design was early the following day and I didn't want to risk missing it, knowing how unreliable bus times were from Zhytomyr to Kyiv.

I crashed at his place and woke up nervous for the day ahead. I hadn't taught a class or given a presentation since the second week of December. I revised my presentation one last time before taking an Uber to the university.

I presented on the intersection of fashion and sustainability. I felt excited, motivated, and inspired by the school and the students. They asked questions, they were curious, and they were engaged. I toured the university afterward, seeing students' projects and craftsmanship. I even saw a fashion collection made of recycled materials.

I thanked the students and professors for their time. I left the university wondering how different my Fulbright experience would have been had I been placed at a university like that, a university where my interests aligned and in a city that was bustling with events, a lifestyle like New York City.

To feel that energy every day would have changed a lot, or so I thought. I grew to love my students and university in Zhytomyr, but I had to fight to align my interests with theirs and the goals of the Philology Department. I walked out of the university and onto the sidewalk. I walked around campus, looking at the skyscrapers around me. If only for a moment, I could imagine this was my daily life.

DÉJÀ VU

Three months after my first trip east to Kramatorsk, I found myself sitting in the same seat, in the same carriage, heading twelve hours back to a city I never thought I would return to. It was near the end of February and the end of my winter vacation; my classes in Zhytomyr would resume soon. Although I could've been resting and preparing for my classes, the opportunity presented itself to go somewhere new, and I jumped on board. I would be spending the next three days on a Fulbright recruiting trip to give presentations and share my experience with students in the East, starting with Kramatorsk.

I arrived at the train station with an all-too-familiar feeling of déjà vu. My previous visit was fueled by personal reasons: my curiosity of what the war-torn East was like and a desire to witness the life my Fulbright friend was living here.

On that trip, I learned that everyone in the city had a story to tell. The barista at the cafe, the teacher at the university, the student in the dorm, the waiter in the restaurant – they all endured the reality of what happens to everyday people in wartime. Their lives were uprooted, their families were split, their friends were lost in combat, and their view of the world likely changed. War wasn't something intangible; it was something that was still happening to them.

I never experienced what the Ukrainian people I encountered lived through. As an American, I have never seen war in my home country. Yet, this was an everyday experience in the East. I wanted to learn more, to meet students affected by the war, and to walk through cities with a direct history of conflict. This trip would allow me to touch the tip of the iceberg, if only for a few days.

The trip would consist of visiting universities and community centers in four formerly occupied cities: Kramatorsk, Slovyansk, Bakhmut, and Kostyantynivka, each sitting about seventy miles or less from the frontline of the war between Ukraine and Russia. For most people, these cities are just a dot on a map, as they were for me. For others, they are cities of devastation, and they are cities of hope. They are cities scattered with shelled-out buildings, displaced citizens, military checkpoints, and soldiers from young to old. They are cities trying to build a unified identity. Yet, at the same time, they are cities filled with cafes, pizza parlors, students learning, and people falling in love. They are filled with people just like you and me: people who love, people who hurt, and people who have dreams. They are a people with a reality many will never live. They are a people with a narrative that only the whispers of war can reveal; a narrative that, if you are willing to listen, shouts beyond the subtle whispers.

As I stepped onto the train platform, I knew I was here to do a specific job, but through that, I told myself I would listen. That's what I needed to do.

PREPARED FOR THE UNEXPECTED

During our recruitment trip to the East, I was part of a group of three Fulbrighters: myself, a fellow English teacher, and a researcher. One of the program directors would be accompanying us. We booked our train tickets individually, set to arrive in Kramatorsk within twenty minutes of one another from our respective cities. We would have a full day of meetings and presentations at the local universities and community centers about Fulbright opportunities for foreigners in the United States. Our program director would lead the presentations and we would be available to share our experience and answer questions.

Thirty minutes before our arrival in Kramatorsk, we received an email from our program director. The email said she was not able to make her train due to health issues and that we would be on our own for the day. She would try to catch a train the following day.

The three of us stood at the train station processing the sudden change of plans, something that happened frequently in Ukraine. We didn't have access to her PowerPoint presentations, nor did we speak Ukrainian fluently to communicate the information written in the presentations. Our worries were put on the back burner as we focused on hailing a taxi to our hotel and looking up the address of the university where we would be giving our first presentation. The researcher headed to a different location; I was the lucky one who had a teammate named Parker, even if I didn't know him that well.

Parker and I arrived five minutes late, wearing jeans, which further conveyed our unpreparedness. We didn't know what we were walking into as we entered the university. We were immediately met by a camera crew from a local TV station. We exchanged a look that conveyed what we were both feeling: "We are so not ready for this." We put our Fulbright smiles on to mask our unpreparedness as we followed a professor I had met on my previous trip to Kramatorsk.

The professor led us to a lecture hall filled with over fifty students around our age, anxiously waiting to hear what we had to say. The camera crew followed us and took their positions throughout the room. The professor informed us that she would be translating and asked us if we were ready to begin.

The two of us stood in the front of the room, wondering how we ended up in this situation. While the professor was giving introductions, we had whispered a game plan to each other and pep talk along with it: we did this every day. He did it in his host city, Kharkiv, and I did it in Zhytomyr. Every day we were surprised by some task we weren't informed about or had to perform on the spot. We gave each other a boost of confidence before we began.

I began, and the words flowed effortlessly and confidently, as did Parker's. When I started speaking about a new topic, he finished and began a new one. We talked about the Fulbright Program, the application process, and our experiences in Ukraine. When he started a new train of thought, I added to it. We bounced off one another; we were a team.

At the end of the presentation, we were individually interviewed by the local TV station. We did what we did during the presentation, pulled it together when we didn't actually have anything together. It was just an extension of our daily life in Ukraine.

After six hours on a train and three hours at the university, we were finally able to relax. We drank coffee with the professor and a few students who attended the presentation. I turned to Parker. I didn't know him well before this trip, but we had both been invited to spend the next few days together doing what we just did. From what he showed me that day, he was someone I wanted to get to know better, and I hoped this trip would allow us to do that. We sipped our coffee and gave each other a high-five. We did it, and we did it as a team.

RUNNING WITH HELP

Grayson's experience in Kramatorsk both matched my experience and contrasted. I didn't live his experience day in and day out. There's a significant difference between visiting a place for a few days and living there for months.

Even in Kramatorsk, one common experience I had across Ukraine was hospitality towards strangers. In Zhytomyr, in Kyiv, in Lviv, and in each new city, I have stories of strangers and friends who extended a helping hand or hospitality towards me.

Before leaving for this trip, I successfully found a gym in Zhytomyr, one that had power, electricity, and techno music. *Who wouldn't want to listen to techno music in Eastern Europe?* The gym was one block away from my flat, which gave me no excuse not to go. That same day, I researched and found a half-marathon in Kyiv scheduled for April 5, six weeks away. I had taken the last three months off from running to give my knees a break. I was eager to start running again and training for my first half-marathon in Ukraine.

I had never trained for a marathon using only gym equipment and a treadmill. Even though I preferred running outdoors, my motivation wasn't high enough to get up early, navigate a running trail in my city or an unfamiliar one, and run in the cold. That was a recipe for failure; the gym would be my second home for the next six weeks.

I found myself laying in my bed in my quiet hotel room in Kramatorsk thinking about two things: 1) It was strange to have a hotel room to myself instead of sharing a dorm with eleven other people, and 2) I needed to find a gym that was open the following morning early enough to get back in time to shower and get ready for a day of presentations.

I messaged Grayson and asked which gym he went to. His gym opened too late; I needed a gym that opened earlier. I found two others and picked the closer of the two.

One plus of staying at a hotel was the front desk service. At 6:30 the following morning, I jogged downstairs and kindly asked the concierge if she could call me a taxi to the gym. I hopped into the taxi, groggy but motivated to start my day with a run, something I hadn't done in weeks.

Twenty minutes later, I arrived at the gym. Nothing is close to anything in Kramatorsk, and this gym was no different. I paid for my day pass and made my way to the treadmill.

It felt good to sweat and get my nerves out for the presentations ahead. I finished my workout and grabbed my jacket out of the locker room – receiving glares for not changing my clothes. Some things never changed. Uber didn't work in Kramatorsk, so I looked up the bus schedule and found a bus that would bring me within ten minutes of the hotel. After waiting outside at the bus stop for fifteen minutes, I gave up. I needed to get back and get ready for the day.

I knew calling a taxi service wouldn't be successful, given my lack of vocabulary, and I didn't see an available one to hail anywhere near. I swallowed my pride and walked back into the gym. I met the same woman who helped me with the day pass. She looked surprised to see me again. I asked her if she spoke English. Two minutes later, I jogged outside with a paper in hand. She had called me a taxi, told the driver the address of my hotel, and had written the license plate number of the car for me so I wouldn't get into the wrong car. It was a good morning: a solid run and a helping hand from a stranger.

ABSENCE

One part of my routine stayed consistent no matter where I traveled within Ukraine and around the world: I always started my day with a coffee. It didn't matter if I made it myself, if I bought it at a coffee stand, or if I went to a cafe. I needed a coffee. It was a small repetition in my life and a little joy that I looked forward to every morning.

It was no different the day I boarded my train to Kramatorsk. I bought a coffee from a stand outside the train station in Kyiv at 5:30 in the morning. A six-hour train ride stood between me and my next coffee that I knew I'd need before the presentations we would be giving there.

"I just arrived in Kramatorsk," Parker's message read.

I asked him if he saw a cafe near the train station that we could stop at before going to our hotel.

He responded, "I'm already on my way to grab a coffee. I'll grab you one too."

I arrived at the train station and saw Parker in the waiting hall, graciously holding an extra cappuccino.

We hadn't spoken much during the previous few months, but I appreciated his positive energy and willingness to do a favor for someone else.

After a day of back-to-back presentations, we called it an early night. I woke up early the next day to go to the gym. After showering, I met Parker downstairs in the dining area to share breakfast. Our server asked us if we wanted coffee or tea.

Coffee was our mutual response. We watched our server pour instant black coffee into our small mugs. We took a sip and read each other's minds; we needed a real coffee if we were going to make it through another day of presentations like yesterday.

I Googled cafes within walking distance to our hotel. The closest one was a generic chain cafe, which was a thirty-minute walk from our accommodation. Beyond that, there were only one or two other cafes within hotels like the one we were sitting in. I had seen hundreds of cafes and coffee stands throughout Ukraine; there are probably hundreds just in Kyiv.

I didn't believe Grayson on my previous trip to Kramatorsk when he told me there was one cafe in the city. *Could there be a lack of something I saw in every other city?* Parker and I drank what was left in our cups, and with each sip, I became more aware of Grayson's life here.

I was determined to find a coffee, even if we didn't have time to walk thirty minutes downtown. There were many times I had surrendered to Ukraine, but not having a morning coffee wasn't a white flag I was willing to raise.

Ukraine could surprise and challenge me at every corner, but not without a morning coffee.

We hailed a taxi to our next destination for the day: Slovyansk. I found a quasi-cafe across from the university where we were giving our next presentation. The "cafe" was a bar and restaurant lounge that looked more like a club than a coffee shop. We had five minutes before our first presentation; time had a mind of its own in Eastern Ukraine.

I bought us two cappuccinos, returning Parker's favor from the train station. We couldn't be late for our presentation again. I chugged the hot drink, queasy from drinking too fast but satisfied that I had a friend who cared just as much about coffee as I did and that Ukraine wasn't taking away my little morning joy.

JUDGING A BOOK BY ITS COVER

We looked at one another as I walked out the door to the left and you walked to the right. The dean was walking Parker to his room for a presentation and his assistant was walking me to a different one. The day before, we had accomplished a day of presentations together without our program director. Now we were going solo.

It's easy to get comfortable when you have good company. I recall the difficult moments I had in the past when I was traveling with a group and our trip came to an end. They would continue to their respective destinations and my solo journeying would start up again. I overcame the fears of being alone when traveling, and I continued to overcome them in Ukraine.

I walked into the classroom, similar to the ones I taught in Zhytomyr: outdated desks and chairs, colorful posters filled with English grammar tips, and maps of the world scattered throughout the room. In every presentation I gave, there was a moment of fear before beginning. *Would my words be understood? If not, would someone be confident enough to speak up and ask me to repeat, explain, or slow down?*

Throughout my education, I was taught that asking questions was a good thing; I shouldn't be scared to do so. I wanted to encourage my students to embrace this mentality, and I hoped the students in front of me had a teacher who felt the same.

I stood before a room of forty students and gave my presentation on the Fulbright Program, my experience of being American in Ukraine, and my research on the intersection of fashion and sustainability. I paused at the end and asked, "Does anyone have any questions?"

The room filled with voices, one question rising after another. The questions began simply, fueled by curiosity about my background and impressions of Ukraine, and soon transitioned to life and motivation.

The voices speaking were confident English speakers, not fearful of making mistakes, not lacking in vocabulary, and not afraid to ask questions.

I judged the students before I stepped foot in that classroom. Through my fear of not being understood, I based my judgment of them on their geographical location and how I perceived that would affect their English proficiency. I saw them as students who were displaced by a war in their hometowns, assuming that the resources they had, if any, were lacking in comparison to other parts of the country and that their priorities didn't rest in learning a foreign language.

I was incredibly wrong. Despite the displacement that many of them had endured in their lives, they were some of the most inspired, engaged, and inquisitive students I met in Ukraine. Their thirst to know more and to share in a conversation inspired me to challenge my presumptions and ask questions the way they did.

I walked out of the classroom and heard whispers of a dialogue I had expressed days before: *As I stepped onto the train platform, I knew I was here to do a specific job, but through that, I told myself I would listen. That's what I was here to do.*

To ask questions, I needed to listen first.

SLINGSHOT

Kramatorsk and Slovyansk had their depressing features, some of which I wasn't sure were the result of being formerly occupied. Maybe everything in a city changes after occupation because the people themselves change. I often wondered this on my trips to these cities. I wondered if, when trying to rebuild their cities after occupation, the people were trying to recreate their original cities, or if they were trying to mold them into something new. *Could a city recover from the effects of war and return to how it was? Were Kramatorsk and Slovyansk always like that?*

I don't know the answer to these questions. It would take much longer to understand the dynamic history of these cities than just a few days in each place. Regardless, after meeting students in each city, the layers of the cities' past seemed to shed. I knew I was still close to an active war, but my feelings had shifted from fear to a feeling of normalcy in these places.

The feeling of fear slingshot into the pit of my stomach just as fast as it had left. On the last day of our trip, we hailed a taxi from our hotel in Kramatorsk to the city of Bakhmut, about an hour's drive eastward. Our program director had arrived. She sat in the front seat, and Parker and I sat together in the back.

The grey city of Kramatorsk faded into the background. As we drove further east, shelled-out buildings appeared one by one, reminiscent of an active war ground. As we passed each one, our program director told us stories of the war and translated others from the local taxi driver.

I listened intently. There was nothing I could say in response to the sights we passed and the stories we heard.

The taxi slowed down, forcing me to shift my gaze to the front window. Five or six cars and a passenger bus were in a line ahead of us. At the front of the line, I noticed a small cement shelter on the right. Two men stood outside the shelter, dressed in military uniforms and holding machine guns braced across their chests. Another man in uniform walked from the first car to the second, also holding a machine gun. I made eye contact with Parker.

After a few minutes, our car was next in line. The taxi driver pulled up slowly to the soldier and stopped. I held my breath as the driver rolled down his window. Our program director had told us not to speak; she and the taxi driver would do the talking.

The soldier waved us forward.

My heart pounded as we drove past him and the other men near the shelter. I released my breath. We were not in danger; it was a Ukrainian military checkpoint, one of many along the route to the frontline. Yet, to be foreigners near a war zone, to be so close to guns that could kill you in an instant was off-putting.

We drove through the outskirts of Bakhmut, nearing our destination. I looked at the apartment buildings, the storefronts, and the restaurants, thinking of the people inside. I wanted to leave, to be far away from this place. As we neared the university, I thought of the students.

That thought was all I needed to keep moving forward.

NEVER-ENDING HAPPINESS

We arrived at our final university, a displaced university in the formerly occupied city of Bakhmut. The city sits about twenty miles from the frontline of the war. I had been nervous on my first trip to Kramatorsk in November, but this was a different kind of nervousness. Seeing shelled-out buildings and being so close to the conflict couldn't be ignored; it was more than nervousness. It was fear.

We went through the motions of our usual presentations as we had done for the previous few days. At the end of the sessions, we opened up for questions.

"Are you always this happy?" a student asked.

The question reverberated in the space between her and me. *Was I putting on a show in front of these students that made them think I was always happy?*

On the surface, I understood why she asked me this: I always smiled in the classroom. My smile was my friendly (and very American) way to communicate with students and create a welcoming atmosphere. Plus, I smiled because I loved my job.

I responded to her question by saying just that: I smiled because I loved teaching and living a life of adventure.

What she didn't know is that her question triggered me.

No, I wasn't always this happy. In fact, I had been living a painful life for many years before this moment.

In 2012, as a high school student, I experienced the worst depression I have ever had. I didn't see hope in the world around me. I couldn't keep up with the pressures of getting top grades, taking exams, and planning for college.

In 2013, my then-eighty-seven-year-old father suffered from a stroke. He spent weeks in a rehabilitation center where he had to relearn how to do basic actions like walking, eating, and getting out of bed. I was seventeen years old when I realized that our roles had switched: he would no longer be taking care of me; I would be taking care of him.

In 2014, I started college. During my first semester, my brother, a second father to me, was diagnosed with stage four pancreatic cancer. Just three weeks later, my father was diagnosed with colon cancer. I didn't think life could get any more painful than the thought of losing the two most important men in my life at the same time.

In 2015, my father became physically disabled. His surgery to remove the cancerous tissue had caused great stress on his body. While he recovered from the surgery and was cancer-free, he would remain in a wheelchair for the rest of his life.

In 2016, my brother died from pancreatic cancer. I held his

hand as he breathed his last breath and slipped from this life to the next, taking a part of my heart with him.

No, I wasn't always as happy as I was standing in front of that classroom. It was in working through those painful realities that I matured in my relationship with happiness. I understood that life would never be filled with only happy moments, but that the moments of pain and suffering define what our happiness looks like. In those painful moments, I held onto the hope that I could come back stronger and smile for others going through their own difficulties. I learned to be reflective in my moments of distress, to rest on my faith and the support of loved ones, and to never lose hope in the beautiful gift of this life. I was happy in that classroom because of what I endured in years prior; I was happy by choice.

ROUND TWO

We finished our presentations at the university around 2:30 in the afternoon. Our respective trains were departing from Kostyantynivka, a city about thirty-five minutes away from Bakhmut – and thirty-five minutes closer to the frontline. We said our goodbyes to the program director, and Parker and I planned what time we should leave Bakhmut to get to the train station.

I prefer to be early, whether it's a train, a taxi ride, or a plane. I would rather sit in an airport or train station for an hour if it means not being crunched for time.

My train was leaving at 4:15 and Parker's was soon after. I wanted to be at the train station thirty minutes early so I could rest easy knowing I wouldn't risk missing my train. Add a thirty-five-minute drive and a military checkpoint to that; it was reasonable to want to leave a buffer of time.

We were eating pizza with two professors and a few students as the clock neared 3:15. I kindly asked one of the professors if she could help us arrange a taxi to Kostyantynivka and soon enough Parker and I were on our way.

A familiar concrete shelter appeared in the distance. Guards with the same military uniforms and machine guns surrounded the area. Earlier that day, we made it through a checkpoint on our way to Bakhmut. It was nerve-racking enough to go through a foreign military checkpoint with our program director who was fluent in both Russian and Ukrainian, and even more so to go at it alone.

Thankfully, Parker's level of Russian was high, but it would still be obvious by our accents and passports that we were Americans. Without our program director with us, we feared we would be questioned further as to our reason for visiting this part of Ukraine.

The taxi driver pulled up slowly, just as before. Parker was in the passenger seat this time and I was in the backseat again. The taxi driver spoke to the guard. The man in military uniform walked from the driver's seat window to the passenger side where Parker was, his gun secured across his chest and a black ski mask over his face.

Parker spoke to the guard and we handed over our passports. At that moment, I was sure we were going to be questioned and was ready to call our program director if something went wrong.

Our passports were back in the safety of our hands as the car began moving. We drove over dirt roads with crater potholes before arriving at the greyest city I have ever visited: Kostyantynivka. I said a meaningful goodbye to Parker and left from the last train station before one passes into the occupied territory. I could leave it all behind, but there were people here who couldn't do the same.

GIFT OF FRIENDSHIP

For many reasons, I was nervous when we arrived in Kramatorsk a few days prior. Sure, I was nervous about traveling through different parts of Eastern Ukraine, but there was something I was even more nervous about.

The company.

Parker and I had hardly spoken during the last six months. I met him for the first time at our orientation in Kansas in July. I had flown twenty-seven hours from Lviv to Kansas to attend our orientation. I was jet-lagged for the entire week. I didn't go out and I didn't spend time getting to know my cohort. Being at that orientation was the last place I wanted to be.

A little over a month later, I met him again at our orientation in Kyiv. I didn't go out and I didn't spend time getting to know my cohort. Being at that orientation was the last place I wanted to be.

Group meet-ups like orientation aren't my cup of tea. I shy away from big groups, not wanting to talk much or put myself in situations that drain me quickly. I like to stay back, gather myself, and get to know people slowly and intentionally.

Parker is friendly, outgoing, energetic, spontaneous, and talkative. He can make friends with anyone, he can party all night, he can laugh and joke, and he can be confident in big groups. He's the kind of guy that thrives at orientations.

When we met up at our conference in October and for Thanksgiving in November, we chatted, but not much. He was one of two people in our Fulbright group that I just couldn't get to know. Our conversation never went beyond small talk.

I would be spending three days, from morning to night, with a guy who I couldn't get beyond small talk with.

That's the thing about Parker; he can talk to anyone. There wasn't a dull moment in our conversations or our experience throughout Eastern Ukraine. Through car rides, checkpoints, and presentations, he was patient with me as he got to know me and I got to know him.

I learned a lot about Parker, about his past, his new fiance, his studies, and his experience teaching in Kharkiv, another city in Eastern Ukraine. I learned about his love for good coffee and good food. I learned about his experience in Ukraine the summer prior and about his interest in international travel.

We had far more in common than our previous conversations suggested.

Parker is the kind of friend who will be there for you during difficult times; he's no stranger to loss and grief. He's the kind of friend who will do something goofy to make you laugh during sad times. He's the kind of friend who will smile with energy and zest for life even when nothing seems to go to plan.

Our trip to the East opened my eyes in many ways. I undoubtedly gained a valuable perspective on the people living in these cities. That was anticipated. However, there was one unexpected gift that trip gave me: a friendship with someone I could count on for weeks and months to come.

FROM ONE TO ANOTHER

After five days in Eastern Ukraine, I felt a mix of inspiration and fear. There was great opportunity in visiting the East: I heard personal testimonies, met inspired students, and saw possibilities for growth at each university. A part of me wanted to continue to be involved in their narrative, yet another part was calling me to the comfort of my home, Zhytomyr.

Zhytomyr would have to wait because I was on a train westward, 150 miles from Kostyantynivka to Dnipro on February 20, the first destination on my way to Mariupol, another previously occupied city.

This time I wasn't participating in a Fulbright outreach trip or working; I was meeting a Fulbright friend, Madeline. She was placed in Mariupol, a city located in the southeast corner of Ukraine. To put the distance in context, it would take about thirty hours by train to get from the village where I taught English in 2018 and 2019 to Mariupol, traveling over 750 miles.

I wanted to visit Dnipro for travel purposes. Madeline and I had been planning to meet for a few weeks, but getting to her city from Zhytomyr would take twenty-one hours. Meeting in Dnipro was our perfect middle ground, since I was already in the eastern part of the country.

I arrived in Dnipro around eleven o'clock at night. There was a sense of ease and excitement to being in a new city.

Even though it was dark, I could tell the city had life to it, reminding me of Kyiv.

I ordered an Uber to the hostel. My rule when traveling solo is to never walk alone at night in a new city. Saving money or trying to figure out directions on your own is not worth the stress, add attention, or risk.

I still remember the name of the hostel: Hostel Smile. The woman inside greeted me and showed me to the mixed dorm room. A set of neatly stacked sheets was placed on my bed. The woman smiled as she handed me a new set, removing the other set from my bed as if she knew they had been there for a while. She turned to leave the dorm room and turned around, saying, "You have a beautiful smile."

I laid in my bed, finding peace as I let my thoughts drift to what tomorrow would bring. It was midnight when the door opened. Madeline arrived, tiptoeing so as not to wake our neighbors up. We whispered our hellos and excitement at seeing one another before calling it a night.

We explored the city all day – visiting churches, walking along the river, admiring the development, drinking coffee and tea, and surprisingly eating Indian food.

It was a fun day with a fun friend, but it wasn't all fun and games. We decided to visit the ATO Museum, a museum about the war between Ukraine and Russia. I heard personal testimonies of the war in days prior, but visiting this museum was a sort of culmination that I needed to experience.

I walked out of the museum feeling nauseous and light-headed. The museum was far more graphic than I had anticipated. There were stories of occupation in Kramatorsk, Slovyansk, and Mariupol: all cities I had visited or would soon be visiting. It was powerful, it was informative, and it was necessary.

We swung our backpacks over our shoulders, said goodbye to the irony of Hostel Smile, and boarded our overnight train to our next destination: Mariupol.

BEACON OF HOPE

We awoke to a grey sky at six o'clock in the morning on February 22. There was a sliver of pink on the horizon before it too turned to greyness. Another winter day in Ukraine and another adventure awaited us.

We stepped off the train platform and onto a crowded marshrutka. *Here we go again,* I thought as we stood in the crowded bus. Mariupol sits approximately twenty miles from the frontline. I assumed the city would exude the same feelings as Kramatorsk, Slovyansk, and Bakhmut.

My eyelids were heavy from our long overnight train from Dnipro, but I kept my gaze glued to the window as we passed shelled-out and bullet-ridden buildings. Despite the physical signs of war, there were trendy cafes and restaurants, development, new construction, and people walking with a different air about them.

I turned to Madeline, expressing my surprise at the difference between Mariupol and the other war-affected cities I visited. Maybe I was comparing apples to oranges; again, I didn't know what Kramatorsk, Slovyansk, Bakhmut, and Kostyantynivka looked like before the war.

We arrived at Madeline's cozy and welcoming flat and sat around her small kitchen table, drinking coffee and tea. As we talked, I commented that it was always so exciting to visit a friend and a new apartment. To think that I had Fulbright friends in different cities across Ukraine who each occupied their own little apartment and lived their own lifestyle. *When would I have the opportunity to have a community like that again?*

Fighting our sleepiness, we decided to venture to a local cafe and start exploring the city. Madeline showed me around the modern, up-and-coming city, a gem hidden in southeast Ukraine.

We visited cafes, co-working spaces, and Madeline's university. We met her colleagues who drove us to see parts of Mariupol outside the downtown area: factories, the shoreline, and a military base.

A familiar gated checkpoint came into view. From the stories I heard, those who are allowed to pass through the route beyond the checkpoint can spend days in "no man's land" before being let through to the occupied side. As we drove past, I imagined people who worked, who had family, who had to bring money and food to the other side. *Had their fears been erased or was there always a relenting sense of uncertainty when crossing over?*

Madeline and I imagined what it would be like to see Donetsk, a major city in occupied territory, a place if we visited would render us an immediate suspension of our Fulbright grants and a return to the United States. Donetsk was the financial capital of Ukraine. I wondered about the buildings there, if there were skyscrapers. I wondered about the universities; many displaced universities I already visited had a duplicate on the occupied side. I wondered about the destruction and the pace of life of the people who lived there.

I looked in the rearview mirror, my eyes glued to the

checkpoint. It faded into the distance as the busyness of downtown replaced it. Mariupol was an unlikely tourist destination, but to me, it was a beacon of hope and of transformation for a post-war Eastern Ukraine.

THE GREAT CHASM

One divide was more apparent than ever after traveling in Eastern Ukraine for a week: the chasm between Ukrainian and Russian languages.

During my time teaching near Lviv, I was exposed to patriotic testimonies of Ukraine. Most of my students were from Western Ukraine, a region fueled by a common passion and drive to preserve Ukrainian culture and language.

Having close relationships with these students led me to fit under their umbrella for two summers: I believed all people should speak the Ukrainian language in Ukraine. My students initially motivated me to pursue Ukrainian language studies instead of Russian during my Fulbright. After all, Ukrainian is the official language of the country. From my experience, there is a sense of taboo in speaking Russian, the language of the people that the country is currently in a war with, or an assumption that you are taking the side of the enemy if you speak Russian.

However, my perspective expanded during my time living in Zhytomyr, a city located in the middle of the country where locals speak Russian, Ukrainian, and a mix of both languages, often referred to as "Surzhyk."

After living in Zhytomyr and traveling to twenty cities across the country, especially cities in Eastern Ukraine where Russian is widely spoken, I learned that the battle of the languages was much deeper than simply enforcing an "official language" of the country.

In places where Russian is spoken, some people are undoubtedly pro-Russian. Yet, in other places where Russian is spoken, people simply speak Russian because it's the language that their families grew up speaking (or were forced to speak) and it's the language that is still spoken in their homes.

I've met some Ukrainians in Eastern *and* Western Ukraine who say it's possible to speak Russian and still be pro-Ukrainian. At the same time, I've also met some Ukrainians who won't even respond if they are spoken to in Russian.

The language divide is unlike any country I've visited; it's full of debate and charged meaning for different people. From a foreigner's perspective, it's challenging to walk the fine line of choosing not only which language to study, but also which language to speak in which place.

I now look at the divide from a surface level of language as a form of communication and have since started studying Russian for its widespread usage. Yet, there is a little nagging voice in the back of my head that still wants to study Ukrainian and speak it when I return one day. I don't have a correct answer or a political stance. What I do have is a thought-provoking experience in a country that is divided in its national identity, language, and culture – an experience that will take more than nine months to understand.

MOTION

My weekend in Mariupol was coming to a close. I had been traveling for nearly two and a half months, since my university was closed for winter break. My biggest journey was still ahead.

Twenty-one hours stood between me and Zhytomyr.

I chickened out on my first trip to Mariupol for many reasons, one of them being that I was afraid to commit to an eighteen-hour overnight train ride from Mariupol to Kyiv. No phone service, hit-or-miss cabin temperatures (you freeze or overheat), and motion sickness. You get the idea.

I hugged Madeline and her colleagues, thanking each of them for their hospitality and for showing me their city. I boarded the train at five o'clock in the evening and walked through the cabin. I booked a third-class ticket as always, which meant I would be sleeping in the same cabin as sixty other people. I found my bottom bunk and looked around to see who my bunkmates were.

What does a person do for eighteen hours on a train?

I read my Kindle.

I journaled about my winter travels.

I ate peanut butter, chocolate, and a granola bar.

I day-dreamed about a boy, ideas for presentations, and exploration.

I slept through the bumping, swaying, stopping, and going.

Before I knew it, the train was slowing down and the conductor announced our arrival in Kyiv. I smiled as I folded my bunk bed into its original position: a chair and table. I packed my belongings, washed my face, and smiled to myself. I did it.

My journey wasn't over yet. I walked ten minutes to the nearest bus station, where I would need to wait for the next bus to Zhytomyr.

I found the bus labeled Zhytomyr, grabbed a quick cappuccino, and boarded.

Three hours later, I arrived in my flat. It was the morning of Monday, February 24, around eleven o'clock. I set my bags down as I received a message from one of the professors, "Can you teach a class today?"

My bags remained unpacked, my refrigerator empty, and my body stiff from an uncomfortable night's sleep.

I stopped for another cappuccino on my way to the university. It was Monday, after all.

STUCK IN PLACE

One of my goals for the year was to visit each of my eight colleagues in their host cities. By the end of February, I had visited five of them in their respective cities: Kramatorsk, Chernivtsi, Ivano-Frankivsk, Ostroh, and Mariupol.

A southern Ukrainian city was next on my list: Mykolaiv. My Fulbright friend, Scarlett, was hosting a professional development workshop at her university and asked our cohort for volunteers to give presentations on resumes and cover letter writing. Combining my visit with the opportunity to provide a resource for students had me eager to book a ticket.

I journeyed two hours by bus from Zhytomyr to Kyiv, and then an additional twelve hours and 300 miles from the capital south to Mykolaiv. Awaiting me were my two Fulbright friends, Scarlett and Grayson.

It was a Thursday morning when I arrived. I had packed my classes on the frontend of the week so that I could have the opportunity to support my friend's workshop. Just as I arrived, Scarlett rushed out of her apartment on her way to her morning class, which she didn't want to be late for.

Grayson and I were left in her apartment, enjoying the slow morning and a break from the busyness of school I was adjusting to again after winter break. We ate breakfast, went out for a coffee, and walked to her university to prepare for the afternoon workshop series.

The workshop was successful; we worked well together and the students were participative. It was a long afternoon that turned into an evening and dinner with new friends and conversation.

After dinner, we ate chocolate and sipped tea, sitting on rickety plastic stools around Scarlett's tiny kitchen table. We did what we always did when we were reunited with one another: we shared memories and updates of our lives since we last saw each other, usually resulting in laughter, meaningful conversations, or debates.

I don't remember which of those was happening at that moment, but I do remember the laughter at what happened afterward.

Grayson's tiny chair slid from underneath him, and, somehow, his bottom half was stuck in the underside of the chair while his legs and arms were free. He wriggled on the linoleum floor, but the plastic legs of the chair held a tight grip on his butt.

Tears flowed out of my eyes. I couldn't see clearly; the more I laughed the more my vision blurred. Scarlett was in the same position, bent over from laughing. We couldn't stop the laughter that flowed from that kitchen.

We helped our friend up from the floor through the laughter and asked if he was okay. Our tea was cold, and even if we wanted to drink it, we couldn't get through a sip without another bout of laughter.

Sometimes, no matter how hard you try, you get stuck in life. Maybe you get stuck because of the decisions you make, because your expectations don't align with reality, or because you take life a little too seriously. Laughter was a remedy that night, even for the one with his butt stuck in a plastic chair.

A CENTER FOR CHANGE

There was another reason I wanted to visit Mykolaiv: Scarlett was involved in special education. Before her Fulbright, she worked in special education advocacy in New York City. Now, she was researching special education development in Ukraine and working with a Ukrainian colleague, Dima, who had completed his Fulbright Master's degree in Child Development.

It was Saturday, February 29, a leap year. Grayson had taken a morning train to Kyiv; Scarlett and I would have another busy day ahead. We would be spending the day visiting a disability center two hours from Mykolaiv in the town of Vosnesensk.

I remember feeling very sick the night before. I missed dinner and drinks and went to bed earlier than usual.

Either I caught a bug or I was overexerting my tired body. Travel all you can and to your heart's desire, but take care of yourself and your body. It's the vessel that allows you to see and experience these places.

Dima picked us up at Scarlett's apartment. His friend was already sitting in the front seat of the car and another woman was in the back. I later learned that she was a Fulbright Scholar teaching Psychology at the same university as Scarlett. She would be presenting on cognitive behavioral therapy for children with autism.

We drove through village after village. I was grateful that I didn't feel as sick as the night before, but I still wasn't feeling 100 percent. I was excited to see this one-of-a-kind center: a specific resource for disabled children and support for their parents.

The building was simple, exactly how I imagined it would be. The main room was filled with parents, maybe forty people. The Fulbright Scholar ran the presentations for the day. Scarlett and I simply added tidbits of our experiences working in special education in the United States. Scarlett had more experience than me; I was far from qualified to give a detailed presentation on special education. I simply shared moments of my time working with disabled students.

The parents absorbed every word. My job as a teaching assistant for children with disabilities and Scarlett's job as a special education advocate didn't exist in the same capacity in Ukraine. There was a sense of hope that filled the room, a hope that these jobs could one day exist in all corners of Ukraine. Yet, there was also a sense of heaviness and grief. These parents were battling a system that left their children with limited resources and support.

To know that some people have that much pressure on their shoulders – to take on the roles of caretaker, educator, and advocate with limited government, educational, or health support – left me with a feeling of heaviness, a sort of communal grief. I imagined my father, a man physically disabled, bound to a wheelchair, and partially deaf. *What would his life be like if he was in Ukraine? Would he have caretakers to help him dress each day? Would he have the technology to hear our voices? Would he be able to leave his house and navigate in a wheelchair?*

I could have spent a year just volunteering and learning about special education advocacy and development across Ukraine. Visiting that center touched my heart with drops of grief, sadness, hope, and gratitude. I would never live the lives of the parents we met, but I would return to the United States and see my father's caretakers, his health team, and the technological resources that allowed me to communicate with him in a new light of gratitude and debt to those who helped paved the way for disability advocacy.

A BLACK HOLE

This book wouldn't be complete without addressing one of the least enjoyable things about traveling in Ukraine: the squat toilets.

For those of you who haven't had the experience of using a squat toilet, in my opinion, it's one of the most challenging and inconvenient ways to use the bathroom, especially if you're a woman. A squat toilet is literally a hole in the ground. Squat and try to aim. Some have a flusher and some don't. They are common in most public restrooms in Ukraine (and in many other countries) and are unavoidable unless you strategically plan your bathroom habits.

I can tell you which restaurants and cafes have sitting toilets near the train and bus stations in Kyiv and which restaurants and cafes have sitting toilets near my university in Zhytomyr. I can even tell you the secrets of surviving squat toilets through many corners of Ukraine.

My first experience with a squat toilet was in China in 2016. I opened the bathroom door and shut it as quickly as I opened it. I had never used a squat toilet. *How does one make it in the hole?*

I hadn't seen a squat toilet in Ukraine until I arrived at my university in Zhytomyr. I was meeting with the dean to review my goals for the year. I was dressed up and wearing summer heels; I wanted to make a good first impression.

After our meeting, I needed to use the restroom. I walked into the women's bathroom and opened a stall door, only to be met with my very first squat toilet in Ukraine. I shut the door as quickly as I opened it. I thought I was going to pee my pants all the way back to my apartment. It didn't matter to me if I did; I couldn't use a squat toilet while balancing in heels.

For the next two weeks, I tried every cafe within a two-block radius, scoping out each of their bathroom situations. I found a cafe one block away that had a sitting toilet. With my twenty-minute break between classes, I could power walk to the cafe, order a cappuccino, use the restroom while I was waiting for it, grab my coffee, and be back just in time for class. I also forgot to tell you that most squat toilets in Ukraine don't come with toilet paper.

I successfully avoided the toilet at the university for the duration of my grant. Avoiding the squat toilets at bus and train stations across Ukraine was the next challenge. In Kyiv, it was easy. There were cafes in every direction. As long as you didn't drink a ton of liquid on the bus or train, you'd be okay. I also forgot to tell you that public squat toilets in Ukraine come with a small entrance fee for usage.

Avoiding squat toilets in new cities was the biggest challenge. Not knowing the surrounding area often left me with a heavy backpack and a full bladder. I usually made it to my hostel or a cafe in time. However, other times I wasn't so lucky. I can count the number of times that my luck ran out and I had to use a squat toilet. I also forgot to tell you that there are no hooks for your bag or coat in the stall. I'll say a prayer for your balance as you squat, lift your coat, and try not to overbalance with the weight of your backpack.

The secret to the squatty potty is to grow up using one: you have a secret talent that others don't have. If you are not used to squat toilets, the secret is to be a man: you can aim perfectly and you don't have to go anywhere near the hole. If you're a woman, the secret is to búy a silicon pee funnel: it's a magical invention that allows you to reap the benefits of aiming that men have. If you have to go number two, well, you're shit out of luck.

VISITING A NEIGHBOR

It was the first week of March and school was back in session in full force. I sat on my couch and opened my agenda. Each weekend in March was already filled. The first weekend, I would visit Belarus, the second, Lithuania, the third, Turkey, and the last, Kharkiv for a final Fulbright conference. It would be my most jam-packed month yet.

While I planned to travel for all of the weekends in March, I kept every weekend in April absolutely free. I would stay in Zhytomyr, meet my students for coffee and game nights, and finally see what life was like if I slowed down. I kept saying I wanted to do just that, and I was determined to make it a reality.

It was time for my first weekend trip. I boarded the usual bus to Kyiv and stayed at a hostel near the train station. I didn't ask any Fulbrighters in Kyiv if I could stay with them; I couldn't keep asking for a place to sleep.

I took the train to the airport the following morning at six o'clock on March 6. I sat in the gate area waiting for my plane to board to Minsk. Since Belarus neighbors Ukraine to the north, I wanted to take a ten-hour overnight train from Zhytomyr to Minsk. Due to visa restrictions, I could only fly directly into the capital city without waiting weeks for a visa.

My backpack had gotten its use over the last few weeks, but one thing looked different. I had my sneakers strapped to the outside of my bag, a trick my running friend taught me while we were living in Milan. If you can't fit your shoes inside your backpack, just tie the laces to one of the straps.

I said I would run one half-marathon and one full marathon in Ukraine before I left. There was only one way to stick to that plan: I had to run even if I was traveling.

I was excited to see my friends, two fellow Fulbrighters who were teaching English in Belarus. I had met Leah and Kristen at our conference in Kyiv the previous October. Kristen and I had both been sneaking in a late-night workout session one day during the conference. It must have been nine or ten o'clock at night when we met. We were the only two girls in the gym. I remember it was my second workout of the day; at that point, I was working out to detach myself from my heartbreak and as an excuse not to go out and party. I got off the treadmill and introduced myself, assuming Kristen was also a Fulbrighter. I liked her from the start; she was dedicated to her health, had traveled and lived abroad, and was big on sustainability. We said we would try to meet up over the next few months.

My feet hit the treadmill, one after the other. I was in a gym in Baranovichi, Belarus. Kristen understood my commitment to running. After all, our friendship started in a gym.

I pressed the stop button and the treadmill slowed to a halt. Seven miles done – seven miles closer to completing a half-marathon in Ukraine. Less than four weeks later, I would be running through the streets of Kyiv. I walked outside, my wet hair exposed to the winter air that still lingered. I hailed a taxi to Kristen's apartment, ate Georgian food to my heart's content, and cheered to a successful Belarusian adventure.

OPPORTUNITY

I laid in my bed exhausted, having traveled twelve hours from Minsk to my home in Zhytomyr. The first trip was complete. One down, three more to go. I closed my eyes, thankful for the freedom to live my dream and see new places around the world.

Our holiday vacation lasted almost three months. I walked into my first class, elated to return to teaching after what seemed like an endless holiday. While there were challenging moments of reflection, I enjoyed every day of my time off and wanted to hear all about how my students spent their days, about the places they saw, and the memories they made.

I eagerly asked, "What did you do for three months? How was your holiday?"

They responded, "It was good. We didn't do much. We stayed at home with our families."

I continued pushing, "For three months? Did you travel? Go anyplace new?"

They looked at one another and all gave me the same response, "No." "No." and "No."

I taught seven classes that week. I walked into each class anticipating a different response and eagerly waiting for someone to tell me an exciting travel story. Yet with each class, I was met with the same sullen "no." *Besides taking exams and celebrating the holidays, did they really do nothing for three months like they were telling me? Was I missing something cultural? Did I misunderstand something in our conversation?*

The freedom I had been dwelling on after that trip to Belarus wasn't freedom; it was opportunity. I had a marked sense of opportunity, and that opportunity contributed to the stark contrast between how my break looked versus my students'. I had the means of affording travel that comes with a comfortable salary, which allowed me to pay for all of my trains, accommodation, and dining, to pay for my once-in-a-lifetime snowboard experience, a dreamy spa day, and an intensive language course. I was in a position in my life where I didn't have college responsibilities or a typical corporate job schedule.

While this interaction shed light on each of these opportunities, it would be mistaken to assume that my students would even want the same lifestyle of travel as I was living or to assume that they didn't have the means to travel based on the economic status of their country. They could've been relaxing from a stressful semester of studies and internships. They could've been spending valuable time with family members, something I often caught myself wishing for. They could've been saving money for future travels or other plans.

I don't know the answers to my questions, but I do know that each of my students came from a different background, one that can't be molded into a clear-cut statement comparing one person's opportunity and lifestyle to another.

That's what I missed.

GIRL POWER

Many of these stories don't speak about my teaching experiences at the university. This is a choice I've made on purpose. Although it seems like I traveled most of the time, the reason for that is: 1) I chose to highlight the travel stories to paint a larger picture of Ukraine; writing about Zhytomyr would only be a piece of the puzzle; 2) I can't tell you what my students' experiences were like in our classes; they are the only ones who can speak to that; and 3) I was only teaching full-time from October to mid-December before winter break. (Winter break is often two months or longer at universities in Ukraine due to the high cost of heating the buildings during winter, or so I was told.)

From Monday to Friday, when school was in session, I was committed to my students and to them alone. I did the job

I came to do, and I did it as best as I could. The part of my job that I loved the most was the extracurricular clubs that I launched in early October. I started three clubs: Speaking Club, Business Club, and Women in Leadership (WIL) Club. Each had its own focus, as you can imagine. We met every Wednesday for Speaking Club and alternating Thursdays for Business Club and WIL Club.

I loved meeting with students outside of the formality of class. I could see them a little more relaxed and a little more excited. That's the way I really got to know them.

It wasn't easy to gain momentum and participation in our weekly meetings. The culture at Ukrainian universities is different from American universities where students are often involved in many campus activities. At my host university, students attended their classes and then went home to do their homework. Classes started at nine o'clock in the morning and ended around three o'clock in the afternoon. From my experience, by four o'clock, the hallways were dark and dim.

Encouraging students to come to clubs after a full day of classes was a feat. At first, students thought my clubs were another class in which they would receive homework. After our Halloween party, that misconception began to shift. Food and parties tend to bring people together, even in Ukraine.

Over the next few weeks, participation slowly increased. Each meeting brought up a new topic: entrepreneurship, confidence building, minimalism, and international travel. While each club had its own focus and attendees, WIL held a special place in my heart. Seeing young women come to our meetings and share experiences and conversations not only built up my own confidence, but also provided me with a sense of belonging and community. I hoped it did for them, too.

At one of our meetings in November, I suggested to the girls that we should design a graphic t-shirt together as a symbol of our club. I showed them examples of shirts I was thinking of and asked if anyone had ideas for a design. I suggested that we design and order the shirts after winter break.

I didn't know winter break would be three months, and I didn't know that the world was about to be hit with a pandemic.

It was March 11, a Wednesday. I scheduled our first Speaking Club meeting since returning from break. The room was filled with the highest attendance I had ever seen. I'm embarrassed to admit this, but I falsely assumed our first meeting back from break would just have a few familiar faces, not an entire conference room full. That being said, I didn't have a plan for that many people. However, I did have coffee and food. As I said, food tends to bring people together, even in Ukraine and even if you're unprepared.

That day, we found out that the Ukrainian government issued a mandate that universities would be closed for two weeks and gatherings with over 250 people would be shut down due to COVID-19. We would return to in-person teaching after this short quarantine. The news was big enough to give us plenty to speak about during our meeting.

I thanked each student for showing up, commenting on how grateful I was that the entire room was filled with familiar faces. I thanked them for supporting me as a teacher and as a foreigner in their country. I thanked them for their continued participation and encouraged them to continue to attend throughout the spring semester.

As the meeting closed, we said our goodbyes and "see you

after quarantine." I received hugs and an extra amount of love from my students that day.

I was cleaning up the coffee cups and cookie wrappers when I noticed one of my students waiting for me. She attended my Speaking Club and WIL Club regularly. She handed me a gift carefully wrapped in floral paper and tied with a delicate ribbon.

"Thank you for everything you've done for us so far. See you soon," she said as she hugged me tightly and met up with the other students outside.

I opened the gift in the empty classroom and couldn't stop smiling. It was the white graphic t-shirt that I suggested we make for our WIL Club. She hand-embroidered "GRL PWR" on the shirt in pink and purple thread.

A tear trickled down my cheek as I held the gift in my hands. God had a way of working everything out. The room was the fullest it ever was, a hidden blessing, as that would be the last time I would see her and my students.

MIDNIGHT STARS

It was March 13 – we were supposed to be in Lithuania, but the world had other plans. We had as perfect of a day as we could have. It wasn't perfect because we followed a plan. It wasn't perfect because we talked every second. It wasn't perfect because we had a promise for tomorrow. It was perfect because we had each other, and on that day, I think that's what we both needed.

I woke up at nine o'clock in the morning, later than I had in weeks. It felt good to sleep in. I had taken on responsibilities in and out of school for the spring semester: researching special education, planning a conference at my university, and volunteering at the local library.

It was the start of spring in Kyiv. The sun was shining through the white curtains and the blue sky struck us both. It was a beautiful day, and we were determined to make it more beautiful despite what we feared would happen.

We shared breakfast and you took me to your favorite coffee shop, ordering me a filter coffee. I told you I missed a simple American cup of coffee. It was the closest thing to that. I sat in joy, sipping my drink and letting the sunshine hit my face.

I asked, "What flavor do you think they added to this? I think it's hazelnut."

He admitted, "I never noticed before."

The little things; we noticed the little things that day.

We helped one another, reminding each one not to read the news, the emails, and the messages. The present moment was calling our names. We held onto that as we played tourists in a city we both knew well. We took the bus to the Friendship Arch, walked across the pedestrian bridge, and put our feet in the sand and our fingers in the icy water. We sat in the sunshine, ate burgers and fries, and bought books that we both had been searching for. We laughed, we argued, and we smiled.

You were going home to your place in the world. I was going back to mine. I looked at the midnight sky filled with twinkling stars. My heart ached in my chest at the thought of my new reality. I wanted to be taken away to somewhere far away from here. I closed my eyes and I went there, if only for a short time.

HARD PILL TO SWALLOW

There's nothing but pain and emptiness when all of your goodbyes occur suddenly and shortly. *Where do you begin? Who do you say goodbye to? How do you fit in everything you want to do when there isn't enough time to do it all?*

I'm angry. I'm still angry and I still hold a raw pain in my heart from what happened that weekend. With one email, my job was suspended. My time in Ukraine was over, and my life as I knew it was gone in an instant.

The world was shutting down because of a virus. Borders were closing. Planes were stranded. Lives were changed. It was a situation we never could have imagined.

It was Sunday, March 15, my last day in Zhytomyr. I woke up at six o'clock in the morning, wanting to make the most of every last minute I had in the city that had become my home.

In a few hours, I would be meeting some people to say goodbye. I needed the morning time to myself, to experience the stillness of walking down memory lane, trying to compress and relive each moment spent here.

I did what I did every morning after my first morning coffee in my apartment. I walked to my favorite coffee stand to get a second. It was one block from my apartment and on the way to the university.

I ordered my usual, handing the woman the exact change: one dollar for a chocolate poppy seed pastry and a cappuccino. She smiled at me, something she always did as she knew I was a foreigner. This day would be no different to her as she made my coffee; it was everything and more to me.

She handed me my steaming coffee and pastry. I thanked her and smiled like I always did in return.

I walked away from the stand, tears streaming down my cheeks as they had the day before; I wouldn't fight them anymore. I took a sip of my coffee and a bite of my favorite pastry. I wouldn't return to the stand for my daily coffee the following day. I wouldn't return to the university. I wouldn't walk over the pedestrian bridge. I wouldn't get yelled at by Ukrainian bus drivers. I wouldn't trip over cracks in the sidewalks.

The sky was so blue that day, even bluer than the days before. I wasn't used to that in Ukraine; seeing a blue sky was a special treat, a sign that the day would bring happiness even if it was just a bright sky.

Nothing about that day was bright; it was dark and filled with tears, pain, heartbreak, and sadness. But there was one thing that remained: blue skies.

I took the last sip of my coffee and I knew one thing: in the words of author Paulo Coelho, "When you can't go back, you have to worry only about the best way of moving forward."[1]

A SWEET GOODBYE

There wasn't enough time. There wasn't enough time to say goodbye to my students. There wasn't enough time to clean out my apartment. There wasn't enough time to buy gifts and souvenirs for family and friends.

It was all gone. In forty-eight hours, it was gone.

Iryna was one of the few people I had the chance to say

goodbye to. Saying goodbye to her was non-negotiable: she was the woman who had selflessly taught me Ukrainian for free for the last seven months, the woman who had guided me through my transition as a teacher in Zhytomyr, the woman who kept me fit and active.

Iryna and I met at her new school location, which she had just renovated. It was bittersweet to see a fresh new place ready for students and learning, knowing I wouldn't be able to sit at those desks.

We walked through the city, making our way back to the place we originally met: the market. Iryna weaved her way through the endless stands. Even after seven months of living in Ukraine, I still got lost inside the market. She amazed me even on the last day we saw each other.

I looked at her with more gratitude than I had words for. We stood in front of the stand where she bought the Belarusian milk for Ted. She gave the seller money in exchange for a can of milk. She handed it to me, saying, "It's a gift for your mother."

We hugged each other tightly as tears filled my eyes, knowing it would be the last time we would see each other. I thanked her again and again for all that she did for me; no amount of "thank you's" could be enough.

As she let go, I smiled, saying, "Thanks for teaching me Ukrainian and thanks for calling strangers who speak English."

We hugged each other one last time. I continued alone through the market, making my way back towards my apartment. I passed Larysa's store, smiling and crying.

LEFT BEHIND

Before living in Ukraine, my friends and family would tell you I was a self-proclaimed minimalist. They would joke and say that I minimize my room once a week, constantly asking if the items I owned added value to my life and happily getting rid of those that didn't. They would tell you that I hate clutter and the idea of unused *stuff*.

If you asked the same question to my friends in Ukraine, I don't think "minimalist" would be the first word they would use to describe me. Although I was still minimalist on my own terms, they would probably laugh and say that I was the one who always packed the most whenever we traveled. I wouldn't argue with them because they were right. I packed for different occasions: professional attire for workshops and events, workout clothes for a quick yoga class or a long run, and casual outfits for exploring a new city.

It was Saturday, March 14 – I had less than twenty-four hours to pack up my apartment. I looked around my room filled with *stuff*. I had accumulated more than I thought over the last seven months, and I had no idea where to start. *Should I pack my clothes first? Should I sort my teaching supplies and books? Should I save room in my bags for gifts and souvenirs?*

I stood paralyzed. I can't tell you how long I remained in the same position. I stared into the numbing space between me and the gravity of the room around me. The task of packing up the life I had rooted in Ukraine overpowered me.

I started with my clothes and stopped. Packing up my apartment meant that going home to the United States was real. It represented the reality that I was leaving behind plans that would never come to fruition, a job unfinished, and a people and place I had grown to love even through the difficult moments.

It was March 15. I looked around at my empty apartment. I stood in front of the wardrobe mirror. Two suitcases and a backpack glared at me as I looked at my reflection. I held the gaze of that girl and the power and strength she had within her. She learned something that day: physical stuff doesn't hold power over us. Stuff doesn't define who we are. Stuff doesn't define the people and places we encounter. The clothes, the books, the notes left behind, that stuff didn't matter.

I did the job I came here to do as best as I could. I nurtured lifelong friendships with people who used to be strangers. I joined a community and built memories in a city I didn't choose and a country unlike my own. That's what mattered.

She locked the door behind her and handed the keys over. The stuff in those bags didn't hold power over her, and neither did the emptiness of what she left behind.

A THOUSAND THORNS

I said goodbye to my Ukrainian tutor, yoga partners, nail artist, colleagues, and a few students who showed up at my apartment. I drank my last coffee and ate my last chocolate pastry. I walked through the streets of Zhytomyr one last time. I visited the church, where I was an outsider by my own doing. I packed up my life in two suitcases and left my carefully decorated room exactly how it was.

Numbness is the only word I can use to describe my last

day in Ukraine. When people are in intense grief, a word of advice is often recommended: take each moment in increments. When the reality around you is too painful, just get through each second. When you feel stronger, get through each minute. When you feel even stronger, get through each hour, each day, each month.

I was in the stage of trying to get through each second. There was so much to process in such a short period. I couldn't get my mind to process it, and so I became numb. I would remain in that state for the coming months.

I had no choice but to keep moving forward, to keep pressing on through each goodbye and each "last." The most painful of them all was saying goodbye to Irena, Valery, and Vlada: my Ukrainian family.

It was two o'clock in the afternoon on March 15. My bags were packed and my ride to Kyiv was waiting for me outside. The following day, I would catch one of the last flights to New York City before the Ukrainian borders closed.

Irena, Valery, Vlada and I stood outside my flat as I looked up to the apartment one last time. The space that was once filled with creativity and warmth was now replaced with the vastness of uncertainty and pain.

I didn't have anything left within me but a heart filled with thorns of brokenness. I handed Vlada a notepad and matching pen, a final present to symbolize our relationship that had grown through simple gift exchanges. I hugged Valery, thanking him for all he did to make me feel comfortable and at home in my apartment and in Zhytomyr. It was time for the worst goodbye of them all: Irena.

I hugged her as tightly as I could, the tears pouring from my eyes.

As I gained confidence, you continued to support me. You asked me how my lessons were, eager to invite me to your classes and allow me to teach your students. You asked me about my visits to other Ukrainian cities. You asked me about my family and upbringing in America, and when I was lonely and homesick, you invited me over for dinner and coffee. You didn't just get to know me as the *American,* you knew me for *me.*

In the weeks that turned into months, I found myself wondering how two strangers ended up building a relationship and becoming like family. The only answer I could come up with was kindness.

When I think about Ukraine, I think about those acts of kindness from people that used to be strangers to me, people that welcomed me into their country, their homes, and their lives. I think about how different my experience would've been without those moments. You used to be one of those strangers, and only now do I understand the power of what you taught me. You taught me to be as kind to others as you were to me. That's a prayer I'll keep praying until we meet again.

I got into the car and waved goodbye to my second family, my host city, and the life I built in Ukraine.

TO MY STUDENTS

Dear Students,

As you read these stories, you may still be wondering why I didn't dedicate more stories to my time in the classroom, to our time together. After all, my purpose in going to Ukraine was to teach English, and the classroom is where

I spent a majority of my days. This story is for you, a letter that I wish I had been able to read to you in person when I was supposed to leave in June, not three months sooner.

It is my deepest desire to spend this God-given life exploring this big world and connecting with people just like you. When I arrived in Ukraine, I was fearful of being assigned to a small city called Zhytomyr, fearful of teaching English to students when I had no formal teaching degree, and fearful of living in a place where I didn't know a single person. I arrived at your university lacking confidence and full of nerves. Yet, from the moment I arrived, you welcomed me with open arms and hospitality.

In each class, you filled my heart with so much love, curiosity, knowledge, and gratitude. It was my greatest joy to be able to wake up, teach a full day of classes, engage in meaningful conversations, and get to know each other beyond the classroom. My favorite memories were when we shared laughter and when you weren't shy in speaking with me, inside and outside the classroom. I came to Zhytomyr to be your teacher, but I left knowing that you were teachers to me as I was to you.

You reaffirmed my belief that life is more than a corporate job. You taught me that I could chase a dream that had nothing to do with my college business degree; that I could travel halfway across the world to start fresh and be successful living a life not defined by money or societal expectations. You showed me, by your commitment to your family and friends, that relationships are more important than any amount of good marks or resumes. You gave me something to be thankful for each and every day: a life filled with creativity, engagement, adventure, and community. That's what it was like being your teacher and walking into your classrooms each and every day.

There's a part of me that holds a sense of bitterness and deep pain for not being able to say goodbye to each one of you, to not have had one more class or one more club meeting, one more smile and wave in the hallway. I often wish I had taken more time to spend with you in Zhytomyr. To lose your job, your apartment, your friends, your students, and your life as you know it within just forty-eight hours is a painful reality I had to swallow. *How do you heal from such a significant loss?* Time and faith in our great Lord are the only remedies that have helped me move forward.

I pray a day will come when we will be reunited. We'll make t-shirts for our Women in Leadership Club, we'll drink coffee every Wednesday for Speaking Club, and we'll visit each other's homes to play Uno and card games. These are the moments I dream about when my mind drifts to a place of happiness and hope for the future. I hope there will come a day when we can embrace again in a new light.

Life isn't fair, and I know that very intimately after this long year. I tried to smile in every class and every meeting throughout my time in Ukraine. Smiling is a way to communicate with others, and it's what I did with each of you. I wanted you to see me smile, even when I had a day of burnout, a day filled with surprises, or a day of homesickness. I didn't want to smile when our time ended the way it did. However, my smile was my way of telling you that life isn't fair, but there are always reasons to smile, to be grateful, and to live life as full as you can. Even though I hold pain in my heart, I'll keep smiling, and I hope you do too wherever God brings us.

Love,
Kat

REFLECTION OF HUMANITY

I sat on the floor, numb to the world. I watched people around me start to congregate at our gate. I was flying from Kyiv to Munich on March 16, 2020, three months earlier than I intended to leave Ukraine. My gaze stared into the space between me and them as I desperately tried to align my mind with where my body was going.

Beep, beep, beep. I was taken out of my trance. A cleaning machine stopped six inches away from me. The driver was doing his job. It didn't matter who was in the way.

I stood up, feeling the weight of what had transpired over the last seventy-two hours. It was time to board my plane home. My mind wanted to stay, to run back to my city, return to a simpler time, and relive the memories I had with friends, colleagues, and students one last time. My body started walking. There was no stopping my new reality.

I stood in line for the next plane from Munich to New York City. The sky was blue again. I tried to smile at this glimpse of hope. As I turned back in line, I made eye contact with the girl in front of me. She had a look of sorrow on her face as she tried to force a smile the same way I did. We sighed at the same time. Without words, we both knew the reason we were both about to board a plane to the United States.

We talked for the next hour. She was a student from Texas studying Math and German in Munich. Her semester abroad was cut short and it was time for her to go home. She didn't know what her future academic career looked like. I told her my story: how my job was suspended and that I had to leave within Ukraine within forty-eight hours. She listened attentively as I did for her. It was a rare moment: two people who likely would never have met, sharing the emotions and uncertainties of their lives as if they had known each other for much longer.

We wished each other well and thanked one another for a conversation that left us both feeling more hopeful than before. I took my seat on the plane. It was nearly empty, except for one group of people: young adults just like me. One after the other took their seats, and soon enough boarding completed. We looked around as if glancing into a reflection of our own selves. Soon, people's expressions changed from sorrow to hope as they started talking to their neighbors, asking what happened, where they had been living or traveling, and expressing their sympathy. We comforted one another, realizing we weren't alone. It was a moment where humans were simply being humans. It didn't matter where we came from or where we were going, we were all human and we were in this together.

As the plane took off, I looked out my window at those blue skies. A tear fell from my cheek. I prayed that the life I was flying home to would be a life of human moments just like that.

COMFORT OF HOME

My robe traveled the world with me. When I taught English in Ukraine in the summer of 2019, I was battling chronic stomach pain. Because of this, I had to pack my own food and supplements to last me the duration of the summer camp. One of the items I packed was a vegan protein powder. To blend it, I bought a portable, handheld blender.

We arrived at the camp and began settling in. I was

roommates with Aubrey and our other friend, Callie, was in the room next door. I unpacked all of my food and supplies, including my blender. It sat on my dresser, waiting to be used.

One night, Callie came into our room and asked, "What's the one luxury item you packed?"

No one ever asked me a question like that when I traveled. I had packed as minimally as I could, given how much I was traveling before and after the camp and given my food restrictions. I didn't consider any of the items I packed as luxurious.

We sat in silence for a moment as we all thought about our luxury item.

I spoke first, announcing that my portable blender was my luxury item. Aubrey went next: hers was a box of American fruit snacks that she was storing in her nightstand. We waited a minute before Callie finally spoke.

With a serious face, she said, "My luxury item is a pumice stone."

We burst out laughing. Her luxury item was a rock.

I thought about that moment weeks later as I packed for my upcoming departure to Ukraine to start my Fulbright. I laughed to myself as I thought of the irony of my friend's luxury item: a rock. It was something that, ordinarily, one would not think of as luxurious. It was luxurious to her, not because of the price or the high quality of it. Rather, it was luxurious because of the sense of comfort and relaxation it provided her as she bravely left her home and traveled 6000 miles to teach English in a small village in Ukraine. She left her life behind for a summer to give herself of service to students she didn't know, to live in a country where she didn't speak the language, and to selflessly work countless hours without getting paid. If a pumice stone gave her comfort amidst all of that, then I think anyone would consider it luxurious.

I sat in the comfort of my plush robe in an Airbnb in New Jersey. I was in a strict quarantine for two weeks when the idea of writing a book of short stories came to life for the first time. My robe was the luxurious item that I decided to bring to Ukraine during my Fulbright. It was with me as I moved through the uncertainty and challenges of my everyday life in Zhytomyr, the demands of my ever-changing job, and the teetering balance of maintaining new and old relationships in the context of an unfamiliar culture and lifestyle. It wrapped me in comfort as my new world challenged me, a world that continued to challenge me.

DOUBLE-EDGED SWORD

As a blogger and travel writer, much of my time is spent writing and documenting my lifestyle on social media. The irony of this is that it doesn't bother me when I'm residing in my home or resting between travels. Yet, it bothers me greatly when I'm on the road, a time when I usually have the most to write and share. In the past, I've tried to manage this delicate balance: a balance of being present in the place I'm visiting while sharing it through media platforms as it happens in real life. It's a reoccurring feat that leaves me unfulfilled each time.

I can never achieve this balance because the greatest reward that travel has given me is being fully immersed in the culture, the sites, and the people of the place I'm in. When I look at those same immersions through the lens of a screen, I lose sight and only see part of the picture unfolding before me; the rest becomes foggy.

Isn't the job of a blogger and travel writer to bring their readers along for the journey? Maybe the apparent answer is yes, as some of the most successful travel bloggers in the world manage this balance. But to me, the best stories are written from rewind, from a time when I look back to a moment where the last thing on my mind was my phone. Those are the stories where I was living, the ones that had the most impact.

I read a memoir by a travel writer named Kim Dinan with a quote that provided me with an answer to the dilemma of sharing: "[I] encourage you to share your experiences with friends and family. But only share what you want; keep the rest in your heart."[2]

What you read within the covers of this book is only part of my overall journey with Ukraine. While each story builds upon another piece of the narrative of a young traveler's life in Ukraine, there will always be more. The dilemma I have on each trip persists because there is always a decision to share or to hold my experiences within.

The parts that I held within are a mix of firsts that happen in a new place, of soul-to-soul conversations with friends who were once strangers, of perseverance and self-growth, and of hidden memories that remain in the place they were created. I believe these are the moments when travelers forget about their phone, the moments that remind them why they left the comfort of their home, and the moments that make them want to do it all over again.

Some of the people reading this now will know the stories that I kept in my heart because they were there to live them with me. For others, the only way to know these stories is to go. Go and experience what I've written about and do me a favor: put your phone away, and when you return, keep some stories in your heart for the next time you're on the road.

A FINAL STORY

I sat in that Jersey City apartment for two weeks alone, completely and utterly alone, as the world around me came crashing down. Businesses closed. Storefronts were abandoned. People were grounded in whatever place they now called "home."

It wasn't just the outside world that was crashing; my inner world had tumbled into a sea of blackness. A place of darkness and deep pain, a place where no amount of messages, condolences, and words could reach. I ate, I showered, and I sat mindlessly on my bed. In this place, I couldn't understand how something like this could happen, how I could lose everything I loved in such a short period of time. I had a plan that I was supposed to follow. I wasn't supposed to be in this apartment alone in New Jersey. It wasn't supposed to be like this.

"It wasn't supposed to be like this," I sobbed.

I should've been teaching, visiting the remaining host cities of my friends, and spending more time in Zhytomyr. I should've been able to bask in the joy of springtime and sunny weather in Ukraine. I should've been completing the program I worked so hard to get into.

I should've been able to hug my family when they picked me up at the airport instead of taking an Uber to a city thirty minutes away from them. I should've been able to feel a rush of excitement and happiness for returning home to my ninety-five-year-old father, thankful to have him back in my life.

I should've been anywhere but here.

I walked into my childhood home, wearing a mask and walking straight towards my father's room. I needed to see him, to know that the one thing I still had remained the same: my family.

It was April 1, 2020, exactly one year since I found out I was awarded a Fulbright English Teaching Assistantship to Ukraine.

It was April 1, 2020, the day my father was found unresponsive.

To be in a sea of darkness, that's how I describe having to leave Ukraine so suddenly and to be in quarantine for two isolating weeks. To be in a raging storm of agony and grief, that's how I describe the pain of knowing my father was dying.

My father knew I was home. He knew I was there. Over the next two and a half agonizing months, I would sit by his bedside, holding his hand, blowing him kisses, telling him I loved him over and over again.

In the days he slipped into unconsciousness, I stayed by his bedside sobbing words of prayer and asking for forgiveness – forgiveness that I didn't ask him the questions I knew he would never be able to answer, forgiveness for selfishly choosing to travel instead of being by his side in his old age, and forgiveness for not being a more present and patient daughter.

When I left Ukraine on March 16, I thought I lost everything. I was wrong; I lost everything on June 13, 2020.

My father was ninety-five years old when he passed away. He lives within my heart each day; it is there that the memory of his life and love has begun to free me from the raging storm of agony and grief from his loss. It is the pages of these stories that have begun to free me from the sea of darkness of leaving Ukraine. It is the Lord who has begun to free me from my plan and to show me that there is a plan in place that goes above our human understanding.

I placed a rose on the newly planted grass, the place I would often visit as I was writing this book. My fingers traced over the letters of my brother's name first, then over my father's. Two dragonflies danced in the space between me and my brother and father's resting place. As the dragonflies flew upwards, I traced their wings as they drifted towards the big ocean of *blue skies.*

EPILOGUE

A traveler's dilemma – to stay or to go.

Since returning from Ukraine, I have lived in my childhood home while writing these stories over the course of twelve months, the longest period of time I have remained in one place since starting high school in 2014. Over this period, I have found gratification in spending time with my family. I have also developed a deepened trust in God for allowing me to be home with my father during his last weeks.

Grounding myself has not only given me time with my family, but it has given me time to reflect, pray, and write. For years, I yearned to be a travel writer, but you can't be a writer if you don't make time to write. The slowness of this season of grief (both personal and communal) motivated me to make writing a priority in my life and has pushed me to seek answers to the following questions: *Who do I want to become? Can I support myself through nomadism? What defines success? Are the moments of travel worth time away from loved ones?*

What I can conclude is that, through the gift of an older father and through my many travels, life is more than a career, money, fame, or materialism. I think of life intimately and deeply through the lens of my faith. I value my time and what aligns me with God, including family *and* travel. I won't say "yes" to what the world tells me "I'm supposed to be doing." *What am I supposed to be doing at the age of twenty-five after losing two people who mattered so much to me?* Society tells me to keep pushing onward as fast as possible. Get a new job and move on to the next fix. I will no longer move at the speed of the world; I will move with God, with intention, and with as much authenticity as I can.

Had I moved at the speed of the world, *Blue Skies* would simply remain as memories in the corners of my mind instead of the stories that you've read. I would not have properly mourned the recent loss of my father. I would not have gotten to know my family and friends on a deeper level. I would not have challenged myself to forgive the one who broke my heart.

In retrospect, I can appreciate the blessings that this season of life has afforded me. However, a little voice inside me tells me the life I am currently living is forced, as though I am not meant to be in one place for so long. A sense of longingness remains in my soul: to carry a backpack with just the items I need, meet new people, explore a new place, sit around a bonfire and drink late into the night, and tell stories. I long to sit in an unfamiliar cafe with my journal, a good cappuccino, and a full day of adventure ahead.

Even though my life has changed, I am still a woman of both worlds: travel and home. Whether I remain in the United States, return to Ukraine, or venture to a different country, my sights are set on a new world: a heavenly world where I hope to see the two souls I miss more than any amount of travel…my sweet Poppy and the best "Guy."

To a life of more adventure, faith, and love…cheers and Будьмо!

ENDNOTES

1 Coelho, Paulo. *The Alchemist*. San Francisco: HarperSanFrancisco, 1998. Print.

2 Dinan, Kim. *The Yellow Envelope*. Sourcebooks. 2017. Print.

www.ingramcontent.com/pod-product-compliance
Lightning Source LLC
Chambersburg PA
CBHW030905080526
44589CB00010B/148